'Down these mean streets a
man must go who is not
himself mean, who is neither
tarnished nor afraid.'

Raymond Chandler
The Simple Art of Murder

WATERSTONE'S GUIDE
TO
CRIME FICTION

Edited by Nick Rennison
and Richard Shephard

INTRODUCTION

The aim of the *Waterstone's Guide to Crime Fiction* is, primarily, to offer a generous selection of authors and titles currently available to those readers who enjoy reading novels that fall into the genre, broadly defined, of crime fiction. To this end we have chosen nearly two hundred authors and fourteen hundred titles to include in the guide, which range from the classic English mysteries of Agatha Christie to the brutal crime stories of James Ellroy, from Hammett and Chandler to Ellis Peters and Lindsey Davis. We have been restricted by what is in print in this country. Many authors that we would like to have included are not currently available in the UK or are in print only in the USA. Some authors that we have included have written many books, of which only a few are available. Where this is the case we have listed only those titles which are in print. We have made a very few exceptions to these rules. Either these are authors, such as Simenon, who seem absolutely central to the history of crime fiction, or they are authors, such as David Goodis and John D. McDonald, who are particular enthusiasms of Waterstone's booksellers who have compiled this guide and contributed the brief surveys of writers' works which accompany each entry in the guide.

Despite any restrictions imposed by what is and is not in print, we are confident that the guide provides a wide-ranging selection of excellent crime writing in all the many forms it has taken. The guide is organised alphabetically by author, from Catherine Aird to Margaret Yorke, and each entry is accompanied by a brief account of the writer and the work, written by booksellers and crime fiction buyers from many Waterstone's shops. A separate section, at the end of the guide, groups the authors chosen into smaller sub-genres in order to assist readers in their further exploration of what is a very diverse field. We also include a number of articles and interviews produced for the guide. Lawrence Block and Elmore Leonard talk about their productive careers as crime writers. Nicholas Blincoe examines hard-boiled writing in the UK and Val McDermid looks at the rise and rise of the queer detective. P. C. Doherty offers an explanation for the enormous popularity of historical crime fiction. Most of all this guide is designed to point readers towards new writers and towards writers they might not otherwise discover. If it can show the sheer range and quality of writing that gets shelved in our shops under the heading 'Crime Fiction' it will have achieved its purpose.

JANE ADAMS

Of recent additions to the list of British crime writers, Jane Adams has shown herself to be one of the most gifted and promising. Her first novel *The Greenway* was a haunting and atmospheric tale of a disappearance and the decades-long effect on those left behind. Her second book, *Cast the First Stone*, was a chilling account of paedophilia and pornography in high places.

Cast the First Stone
Pan pbk £5.99 0330350854

The Greenway
Pan pbk £5.99 0330348892

LESLEY GRANT-ADAMSON

For more than a decade Lesley Grant-Adamson has been writing thrillers and mysteries which have been insufficiently recognised as the well-crafted novels they are. Her refreshingly uncontrived plots, set in both town and country, Fleet Street and Cotswold village, and her characters, from con-man to gossip-columnist, are all in the best tradition of English crime fiction but she never lapses into quaintness or sentimentality. She deserves a wide readership.

Dangerous Games
Hodder pbk £5.99 0340628723

Evil Acts
Hodder pbk £5.99 0340660201

The Face of Death
Faber pbk £3.99 0571145183

The Girl in the Case
Hodder hbk £16.99 034066021X

Patterns in the Dust
Faber pbk £5.99 0571145221

Threatening Eye
Faber pbk £5.99 0571153984

Wild Justice
Faber pbk £5.99 0571152821

Wish You Were Here
Hodder pbk £5.99 0340639768

Teach Yourself Crime and Suspense Fiction
Hodder pbk £6.99 0340648163

CATHERINE AIRD

Catherine Aird's gentle and slightly old-fashioned stories, set in an invented English county, are nonetheless genuinely baffling and provide the kind of carefully structured mystery that characterised an earlier era of British detective fiction. Her central characters – the phlegmatic Inspector Sloan and the quirky Sergeant Crosby – are sufficiently engaging to carry the reader through a number of light but entertaining plots.

After Effects
Pan pbk £5.99 0330350722

The Catherine Aird Collection
His Burial Too, Last Respects and Harm's Way
Pan pbk £7.99 0330326457

A Going Concern
Pan pbk £5.99 0330330381

The Second Catherine Aird Collection
The Religious Body, Henrietta Who?, The Complete Steel
Pan pbk £7.99 0330338404

MARGERY ALLINGHAM (1904–1966)

Margery Allingham is one of the great writers of the Golden Age of English crime writers and it is easy to argue that her work has been unjustly overshadowed by that of Agatha Christie and Dorothy L. Sayers. She produced consistently well-written and entertaining mysteries and the crimes she portrays range from murder in an exclusive fashion house (*The Fashion in Shrouds*) to a conspiracy that threatens the security of the nation (*Traitor's Purse*). Most of her books feature her gentlemanly hero Albert Campion, whose affable and frightfully English exterior hides a mind like a steel trap. Campion is aided in his often life-threatening adventures by his wife Lady Amanda, a policeman with the, perhaps, surprising name of Stanislaus and the even more bizarrely named Magersfontein Lugg, Campion's manservant. Despite the overly elaborate and rather stagey characters, Allingham's novels are complex and can be genuinely chilling and sinister. *Tiger in the Smoke*, one of the strangest detective stories of its period, is set against a backdrop of creeping insanity in a London besieged by fog and its denouement remains unsettling. In *Traitor's Purse*, Campion is stricken with amnesia, aware only that he has to remember something vital to the nation. The claustrophobic atmosphere created by Allingham as her hero tries desperately to recover his memory is weirdly compelling and a fine example of the power of this often underrated writer.

The Allingham Casebook Penguin pbk £5.99 0140231528

Black Plumes Penguin pbk £5.99 0140166106

Cargo of Eagles Penguin pbk £5.99 0140166181

The Case of the Late Pig Penguin pbk £4.99 0140087842

The China Governess Penguin pbk £5.99 014016619X

Coroner's Pidgin Penguin pbk £5.99 0140166114

The Crime at Black Dudley Penguin pbk £5.99 0140093818

Dancers in Mourning Penguin pbk £5.99 0140087826

Death of a Ghost Penguin pbk £5.99 0140084231

The Fashion in Shrouds Penguin pbk £5.99 0140166092

Flowers for the Judge Penguin pbk £5.99 0140088350

Look to the Lady Penguin pbk £5.99 0140093796

The Mind Readers Penguin pbk £5.99 0140087788

More Work for the Undertaker Penguin pbk £5.99 014008777X

Mr Campion and Others Penguin pbk £5.99 0140087834

Police at the Funeral Penguin pbk £5.99 014008780X

Sweet Danger Penguin pbk £4.99 0140122435

Take Two at Bedtime Penguin pbk £5.99 014010061X

The Tiger in the Smoke Penguin pbk £5.99 0140166173

Traitor's Purse Penguin pbk £5.99 0140166084

The White Cottage Mystery Penguin pbk £4.99 0140087850

JAKOB ARJOUNI

Anyone familiar with Philip Marlowe's particular form of wise-crack will recognise the model for the dialogue given to Kemal Kayankaya in Jakob Arjouni's three novels, skilfully translated from the German by Anselm Hollo. The intriguing twist is that Kayankaya is a Turkish-born detective, living and working in Frankfurt, who has to contend not only with the usual inconveniences of life as a private eye but also with the racial intolerance of his fellow Germans. Arjouni reflects the reality of a Germany in which Kayankaya, because of his race, can never feel entirely at home and this brings an added edge to the books. In other ways Arjouni's hero is a traditional private eye. He drinks like a fish – Chivas for preference – punches like a heavyweight and follows a case through to its conclusion whatever the effects on his physical and psychological well-being. The plots are all driven by corruption in high places and Kayankaya sees it as his job to cut through the corruption and reach the truth. The books follow a certain pattern. Kayankaya is always at the receiving end of a severe beating at some point in the plot. He is always warned off by the authorities. He is always fired by his clients when his persistence threatens to unearth more than they had bargained for. He always triumphs eventually because of that persistence. Despite the formulaic patterning of the books, they are immensely readable because of the power of Arjouni's story-telling.

Happy Birthday, Turk No Exit Press pbk £4.99 1874061378
More Beer No Exit Press pbk £4.99 1874061289
One Man, One Murder No Exit Press pbk £4.99 1874061297

JO BANNISTER

Jo Bannister was a journalist in Northern Ireland before leaving to pursue her writing career. Her intelligent police procedurals featuring Detective Inspector Liz Graham and her Detective Sergeant, Cal Donovan, have won much praise for their intelligence and humour and for the strength of her characterisation.

A Bleeding of Innocents
Allison & Busby pbk £4.99
0749001461

Burning Desires
Allison & Busby pbk £6.99
0749002824

No Birds Sing
Pan pbk £4.99 0330350447

The Primrose Convention
Macmillan hbk £16.99 0333699610

Sins of the Heart
Allison & Busby pbk £6.99
0749002816

ROBERT BARNARD

Barnard was for many years a lecturer in English literature at universities abroad, particularly in Norway, and has written a short history of English literature which remains in print. He is also a devotee of the classic English detective story and has written a revealing critical study of Agatha Christie. His own fiction is characterised by its skilled plotting, witty dialogue and intelligent prose. Those novels in print reflect the variety of his stories and of their settings. As a reviewer wrote in the *Daily Telegraph*, 'Robert Barnard is always original, never repeats himself and has a delectable wit.'

The Bad Samaritan
HarperCollins pbk £4.99
000649675X

A Hovering of Vultures
Corgi pbk £3.50 0552141194

Masters of the House
HarperCollins pbk £4.99
0006493262

A Scandal in Belgravia
Corgi pbk £2.99 0552136468Z

LINDA BARNES

Every American city should have one – a sensitive, gutsy, feminist private investigator. Carlotta Carlyle is Boston's. Carlotta is a six-foot tall redhead who plays a mean guitar and even meaner volleyball. She shares her home with her cat T. C. and her lodger and, occasionally, employee, Roz, artist and martial arts expert. Between cases Carlotta drives a cab for the Green and White Cab Company which is co-owned by her on/off lover Sam Gianelli. Since Gianelli's family have Mafia connections, he is not popular with Carlotta's old partner from her days in the Boston Police Department, Lieutenant Mooney, whose assistance she still regularly demands. Linda Barnes calls on this disparate band of all too human characters to people her well plotted stories which, whether dealing with the search for a missing writer who, according to police files, was murdered twenty years ago or with an investigation into the dangerous world of illegal aliens, are consistently entertaining and peppered with a pleasing dry wit.

Cold Case
Hodder hbk £16.99 0340597739
Coyote
Hodder pbk £4.99 0340562420
Hardware
Hodder pbk £5.99 0340640219
The Snake Tattoo
Hodder pbk £5.99 0340535385
Snapshot
Hodder pbk £5.99 0340608234
Steel Guitar
Hodder pbk £5.99 0340580356
A Trouble of Fools
Hodder pbk £4.99 0340509198

E. C. BENTLEY (1875–1956)

Bentley was a prolific journalist and a friend of G.K. Chesterton who earned his place in literary history by inventing the light verse form known, after his own middle name, as the clerihew. He earned his place in the history of crime fiction by the publication in 1913 of *Trent's Last Case*, a work which was originally intended as pastiche but which has come to be acknowledged as a classic example of the British detective story of the period. The ingenious plotting and the wryly ironic central character are rooted in a world of upper middle-class semi-bohemia which has long since disappeared.

Trent's Last Case
Oxford UP pbk £4.99 0192824228

NICHOLAS BLINCOE

One of the best and most exciting of young British crime writers, Nicholas Blincoe was born and grew up in Manchester and has worked as a journalist for radio and for newspapers. His first novel, *Acid Casuals*, the story of a transsexual's bloody return to Manchester and its drugs scene, was much praised for its direct prose and for the vigour of its story-telling. His second novel *Jello Salad* is set in Soho in a confusing world of chefs, gangsters and addicts.

Acid Casuals
Serpent's Tail pbk £7.99
1852425091

Jello Salad
Serpent's Tail pbk £7.99
1852425679

BRITISH HARDBOILED
by Nicholas Blincoe

The author of *Acid Casuals* and *Jello Salad* looks at British crime writers who have matched the best of American noir novelists

My kind of writing, the kind that gets called noir or hardboiled or pulp is an American invention. It's a fact. What it shouldn't be is a problem. This is America's century and everything that defines the age has an unmistakable American vibe, whether it's mass-produced cars, cheeseburgers or Rock n'Roll. Today, we're all half-American. What you have to tell yourself is that half-American might actually be better than American. Take Rock n'Roll for example. The first British imitations of Elvis ended in tears, humiliation and Cliff Richard. But, pretty soon, the Beatles came along to ease our shame.

In the world of noir fiction our Cliff Richard is Peter Cheyney. In books like *Can Ladies Kill* (1936), Cheyney uses the first-person to write as tough G-Man Lemmy Caution. Most of the time Cheyney's idea of tough G-Man talk is lifted from the novels of Damon Runyon. The exceptions are when Cheyney simply makes up the slang himself. Either way, the result is distinctly surreal. So surreal that Jean-Luc Godard felt compelled to borrow the character of Lemmy Caution for his artsy French Sci-Fi flick *Alphaville.*

Perhaps Cheyney's problem was that he came too early. As the century has progressed, American has become second nature to British writers. James Hadley Chase, for instance, visited the US less often than Cheyney and still wrote the pulp classic *No Orchids for Miss Blandish.* More recently, Tim Willocks set his storming *Green River Rising* in Texas but only visited the state afterwards, while on tour to promote the book.

Other writers have managed to give British tales a noir edge. Gerald Kersh's novel *Night and the City,* for instance, is a Soho story of an English gangster who, in his language and gestures, is already mutating into a half-American hybrid. When the

novel was filmed, it starred the great Richard Widmark, thereby taking the muta-
tion one step further. A similar gangster tears across Maurice Procter's Manchester-
based novel *Hell Is A City*. This time, though, the gangster plays a supporting role to
the central character, an ex-schoolfriend turned policeman. Procter was an ex-cop
himself and could plausibly claim to have invented the police procedural. Certainly
he wrote his first novels before Ed McBain began his 87th Precinct series. The film
of the novel works by wedding Manchester's half-American good looks with the grit
of the surrounding countryside.

Eric Ambler's *The Mask of Dimitrios* was filmed with Peter Lorre and Sydney
Greenstreet, making it a kind of companion piece to the film of *The Maltese Falcon*.
As the story concerns a crime writer playing a detective, the work can also be read
as a kind of post-modern commentary on Hammett's style of fiction. However
Ambler is even more ambitious than this: as his writer-investigator tramps across
Europe, uncovering more and more about the criminal Dimitrios, he realises that,
far from unmasking a man, he is drawing closer and closer to a devil. Not surpris-
ingly, the book provided the inspiration for Bryan Singer's film *The Usual Suspects*.

The Mask of Dimitrios was originally called *A Coffin for Dimitrios*. The name was
changed to suit the film . . . as was Ted Lewis's *Jack's Return Home* aka *Get Carter*. This
film would be a landmark if only for combining French and American film styles
several years before Scorsese or Coppola. What makes it a classic is the way it uses
this intense style to set a British story in a very British landscape. Ted Lewis's book,
on its own, is not as remarkable. However, all his work, as an oeuvre, makes a mountain that is definitely worth climbing: very tough and incredibly idiosyncratic. It is a
distinguishing feature of crime writers that their work is often better in the long
run.

A literary purist might feel uncomfortable introducing a string of authors
through the films made of their books. But fiction is no place for purists. A novelist
has to be practical . . . which means showing some sympathy for contemporary culture and contemporary pleasures. And if that means using film dialogue and cam-
era techniques, introducing American tropes and dragging overblown phrases out
of tabloids or down from advertising campaigns . . . then so what? A poet or a composer can afford to spend his or her working life pondering abstract or classical
motifs. In a sense their arts are nourished from above, or at least from the past. Not
so novelists. They are nourished from below; meaning, I guess, the present. Take
Defoe, Sterne or Hardy; they were all fuelled by the heady and cheap stuff – pam-
phlets, penny dreadfuls and pulp fictions. And if the novel is going to remain
robust, it needs crime writers: the dark knights who preserve literature's secretly
prurient soul.

Anyone who can produce good hard-boiled noir has to really love fiction . . . love
it even more than their reputation. They can never be the kind of poseur who fan-
cies seeing their name next to Flaubert or Forster on the shelves of the local library.
That kind of writer will never risk his good name producing the bacteria that keeps
the culture of fiction alive.

Derek Raymond, author of the most nightmarishly repulsive book ever, *I Was Dora Suarez*, could be the exception to the rule. Raymond wasn't his real name. It was Robin Cook. Raymond was an old Etonian and one-time bag-man for the Krays who seems to have become a writer as a way of relieving the monotony of self-destruction. His name-change was actually dictated by the market. There was already a writer named Robin Cook (and now there is a Foreign Secretary too).

In the case of P. B. Yuill, a pseudonym was discarded in the interests of the market. Writing partners Terry Venables and Gordon Williams got more coverage for their Hazell series writing in their real names. Williams, a true professional and the author of *Straw Dogs*, has always insisted that Venables pulled his weight by bringing a distinctive up-beat Cockney voice to the novels. So much of the Hazell novels is written in rhyming slang, they're practically in verse. Mark Timlin, author of the Sharman novels, has always acknowledged the professional influence of Hazell as well as the private influence of Derek Raymond.

Now at the close of the twentieth century, in the last days of *l'age noir*, of America's century and the cinema's century, more British writers seem comfortable with crime fiction than ever before. There is Charles Higson's beefy *Full Whack*, Jeremy Cameron's remarkable *Vinnie Got Blown Away*, Colin Bateman's fine (and finely balanced) *Cycle of Violence*, the pulp sociology of James Hawes's *White Merc With Fins* as well as my own dance'n' disaster books *Acid Casuals* and *Jello Salad*. The link between us is humour: comedy and a feeling of ease with the kind of American writing that arrived in Britain ten years ago. Specifically the writing of Charles Willeford, Elmore Leonard and Carl Hiaasen and, through them, the American pulp writers of the forties and fifties – Jim Thompson, Chester Himes and Willeford (again – the great Charles Willeford managed to have two separate careers in crime writing).

For the future, we are going to have to develop new ways to re-connect with contemporary life. The trick is not to get too comfortable, too mannered. Pulp has to be served fresh. I'll be taking a last look at work from the fifties, especially Chester Himes and Maurice Procter, hoping to find something in their confrontation with a rapid-fire post-war world that will help as we career blindly into the next century. Maybe I'm wrong . . . it doesn't really matter. No-one gets blamed for misreading the future. The blame is saved for anyone who refuses to read the present.

Tim Willocks
Green River Rising
Arrow pbk £5.99 0099562413

Charles Higson
Full Whack
Abacus pbk £6.99
0349108110

Jeremy Cameron
Vinnie Got Blown Away
Simon & Schuster £5.99
0684817373

Colin Bateman
Cycle of Violence
HarperCollins £5.99
0006479359

James Hawes
White Merc With Fins
Vintage £5.99 0099591510

See also entries on Ted Lewis and Derek Raymond and Mark Timlin

LAWRENCE BLOCK

Block is one of America's most versatile crime writers. Although perhaps best known for his Matt Scudder novels, featuring an alcoholic and (later in the sequence) reformed alcoholic ex-cop working the mean streets of New York, he has also written a series about the amiable and witty burglar-cum-bookseller Bernie Rhodenbarr and a number of far-fetched capers involving Evan Tanner, who, because of a bizarre military accident, needs no sleep and fills the time he gains by pursuing the sort of knowledge that gets him into a lot of trouble. He has also written a large number of short stories and published work under a variety of pseudonyms.

THE BURGLAR BOOKS

The Burglar in the Closet
No Exit Press pbk £4.99
0948353708

The Burglar in the Library
No Exit Press hbk £14.99
1874061815

The Burglar Who Liked to Quote Kipling
No Exit pbk £4.99 0948353864

The Burglar Who Painted Like Mondrian
No Exit pbk £4.99 0948353635

The Burglar Who Studied Spinoza
No Exit Press pbk £4.99
0948353627

The Burglar Who Thought He Was Bogart
No Exit pbk £5.99 1874061556

The Burglar Who Traded Ted Williams
No Exit pbk £5.99 1874061386

Burglars Can't Be Choosers
No Exit Press pbk £4.99
094835352X

THE MATT SCUDDER MYSTERIES

The Devil Knows You're Dead
Orion pbk £5.99 1857994760

Eight Million Ways to Die
Orion pbk £5.99 1857997255

Even the Wicked
Orion pbk £5.99 075380218X

In the Midst of Death
Orion pbk £5.99 1857994159

A Long Line of Dead Men
Orion pbk £5.99 185799261X

The Matt Scudder Mysteries Vol 1
Orion pbk £9.99 0752805363

The Matt Scudder Mysteries Vol 2
Orion pbk £9.99 0752805398

Out on the Cutting Edge
Orion pbk £5.99 1857993047

The Sins of the Fathers
Orion pbk £5.99 1857994132

A Stab in the Dark
Orion pbk £5.99 1857997263

Time to Murder and Create
Orion pbk £5.99 1857994140

A Walk Among the Tombstones
Orion pbk £5.99 1857993020

When the Sacred Ginmill Closes
Orion pbk £5.99 1857997247

OTHERS

The Cancelled Czech
No Exit pbk £4.99 1874061580

Tanner's Twelve Swingers
No Exit pbk £4.99 1874061688

The Thief Who Couldn't Sleep
No Exit pbk £4.99 1874061548

A Ticket to the Boneyard
Orion pbk £5.99 1857993128

Two for Tanner
No Exit pbk £4.99 1874061793

THE BURGLAR AND
THE BOOZER

Richard Shephard speaks to the prolific American author,
Lawrence Block, about his two greatest creations.

For over thirty years Lawrence Block has been writing superb crime stories and novels, seemingly in a class of his own. From the noirish novels published by Gold Medal and Avon Books in the '60s to the breakthrough Matt Scudder novels conceived in the early '70s to the Bernie Rhodenbarr 'Burglar Who . . . ' series a few years later, Block has produced a hugely impressive body of work.

Probably his most memorable achievement is his invention not just of two utterly different protagonists but of two different fictional worlds: the bleak, cynical universe of Matt Scudder, alcoholic ex-cop and private eye and the relatively sunny world of Bernie Rhodenbarr, the amiable, urbane burglar who, like a modern day Raffles, robs from the rich and gives to himself. Although both men operate outside the law, and possess their own personal, if different, moral codes, it is probably Bernie the thief who seems more law-abiding than Scudder, the ex-policeman. Of the two Scudder is the more vibrant. He is a stunning creation. As an ex-cop in New York he has seen it all. Like many hard-boiled heroes he seems to drift with the tide of circumstances, at least in the early novels. Even his decision to quit the force is due to an accident, albeit a tragic one. While he is pursuing a felon through the streets of the city, there is gunplay. A bullet from Scudder's gun ricochets off a bus stop and kills a child. Although he has killed criminals and witnessed death untold times in his long career as a cop, this chance slaying of an innocent child is too much for Scudder. He hangs up his badge and, more significantly, his gun, leaves his already estranged wife and children and turns his heavy drinking into a full tilt affair with the bottle.

Scudder's alcoholic history is one of the key points of the series and, as the books progress, his drinking increases until, in *When the Sacred Ginmill Closes,* he goes on the wagon permanently. Thereafter, in every book, Scudder attends Alcoholics Anonymous meetings. For a while each book is punctuated by these meetings and the gallons of coffee that Scudder now consumes. Rather than lose their edge, however, the books, if anything, get tougher. In some ways, although Scudder has achieved a certain kind of peace in his sobriety, the bleakness of his world view remains. When we met to discuss his work, Lawrence Block concurred with this : 'In a way, they're actually darker, I think. Going to the meetings is more pronounced right around the time he gets sober and rather less as the series has gone on as he's more secure in his sobriety and he's less inclined to drink.' Similarly a new type of suspense is hinted at, when the reader occasionally wonders if Scudder, under pressure to crack the case, will tumble off the wagon. 'Sure –"Is he going to drink again?". Yes, that was kind of an accident but it works okay.'

The other main series that Block has produced, the Burglar books, has none of this bleakness but relies instead on Bernie Rhodenbarr's irrepressible charm to carry the stories. Despite being a highly professional thief, Bernie has something of the gifted amateur about him, especially when it comes to outwitting the law or other, more dangerous criminals. Popular with the ladies, a light-hearted bon viveur, Bernie steals because he's good at it, because he likes the challenge and the subsequent excitement and also because it's usually more profitable than, and certainly preferable to, working for a living.

By the time the first Bernie book, *Burglars Can't Be Choosers,* appeared in 1977 Block had already written several Scudder novels and the drinking was increasing with each one. One gets the impression that he approached the lighter Burglar books with something like relief, perhaps looking for a humorous antidote to the noir world inhabited by Scudder. To the reader it seems unlikely that there was a transitional period between the two styles and Block himself confirms this. 'No, there wasn't. The actual writing of the first three Scudders was done in 1973–1974 and the first Bernie book was written two years after that and they've interwoven since then. They're very different voices. Occasionally I get asked the question, "Could the two characters be in the same book?" and it strikes me as absurd because they don't live in the same universe. They don't even live in the same New York. Well, Bernie walks on the bright side of the streets, whereas Scudder walks on the dark side.'

With a writer as versatile as Block, the question of influences is an important one. After trawling through the usual suspects, two or three possible names come to mind. Of crime writers, the main one is Donald Westlake. There are many parallels between the two writers, not least the fact that Westlake too has written more than one series and in different styles. One of the series even features a humorous burglar named John Dortmunder. The other series, the darker of the two, written under the pseudonym of Richard Stark, features a thief named Parker (no first name). All the Parker books are excellent and the first, *Point Blank* (later made into a film by John Boorman) is brilliant. Block acknowledges the influence. 'Yes, the parallels are, I suppose, striking. He and I have been close friends for ages. I certainly don't object to comparisons with Don. We've been good friends for close to forty years. What I find surprising is not that he and I write books in several voices, but that more people don't. There are a lot of writers I know with more than one aspect to their personality and I find it surprising that they only reflect one aspect in their work but that's very often the case.'

I suggest the late Ross Macdonald as a possible influence but Block is unconvinced. 'No, I don't think so – but I like his writing, especially in the later books, from *The Galton Case* on. The early books in the series, it seems to me, were very much imitation Chandler and had all the faults of self-conscious imitation but he grew out of that and the books deepened into something that, in some respects, went beyond anything that Chandler did.'

Another strand of literature often linked with the hard-boiled genre is that of the French existentialist writers. Were Camus and Sartre any kind of influence? 'Well, I read *The Outsider* of course and *The Plague*. I don't know if they stayed with me much but that connection between existentialism and American writing is interesting. I read and continue to re-read John O'Hara's work. I'm sure he was an influence as were other American realistic writers of the earlier part of the century.

Amongst the more than thirty novels that Block has written, perhaps the strangest work he has done was the completion of Cornell Woolrich's *Into the Night*, an unfinished work by the master of suspense. Found with other manuscripts after Woolrich's death in 1968, the novel was three quarters finished. Block stepped in to complete the book, including rewriting the first chapter completely, amply demonstrating another side to his talents: a chameleon ability to imitate another writer's very different style. Far more successful than Robert Parker's completion of a Chandler story, *The Poodle Springs Murder*, it was a fine piece of work and, symbolically at least, bridged the gap between two eras of crime writing. ' The task I confronted was this . . . Woolrich did write a full manuscript but it was very much a first draft, at least what survived was. Also the first chapter was lost and there were another 20 or 25 pages missing throughout the manuscript, so I had to fill in the gaps. If I had to do it all over again I think I would be less reverential to what Woolrich had done. His style is very different to mine but I was able to write in it, I think. Robert Parker had enormous reverence for Chandler, much more than I have for Woolrich, but I don't think he was able to match Chandler's style.'

So, whether finishing someone else's work or continuing to produce his own, one thing remains certain. Lawrence Block is the most prolific, original and consistently entertaining crime writers of the past forty years. There's no one to touch him. He's in a class of his own and, quite simply, indispensable.

LILIAN JACKSON BRAUN

Qwill Qwilleran, Yum-Yum and Koko are familiar names to the legions of fans of this author. The writer of the popular 'The Cat Who . . . ' series was moved by the death of a beloved Siamese cat in unexplained circumstances to pen several short stories that featured feline plots and these she promptly sold to *Ellery Queen's Mystery Magazine*. Her first full-length feline mystery *The Cat Who Could Read Backwards* was published to great acclaim in 1966 and the series is still going strong more than twenty titles later. The books feature genial bachelor journalist Qwill Qwilleran whose years in the business have given him a nose for a news story and, more surprisingly, a moustache that twitches and quivers alarmingly when he suspects something is wrong. His sleuthing abilities are aided and abetted by his two Siamese cats, Koko and Yum-Yum, who are integral to the solving of the murders Qwill discovers. The setting of these mysteries is the mythical Moose County and its main city Pickax. The crimes to be solved are deceptively simple but Braun is adept at making the innocuous significant in these frothy whodunnits. The tone of the books is firmly tongue-in-cheek and the reader is invited to share the author's whimsical sense of humour in what are lightweight but pleasing mysteries.

The Cat Who Ate Danish Modern
Headline pbk £5.99 0747250359

The Cat Who Blew the Whistle
Headline pbk £5.99 074724815X

The Cat Who Came to Breakfast
Headline pbk £5.99 0747245134

The Cat Who Could Read Backwards
Headline pbk £4.99 0747250340

The Cat Who Knew a Cardinal
Headline pbk £5.99 0747237883

The Cat Who Knew Shakespeare
Headline pbk £5.99 0747250383

The Cat Who Lived High
Headline pbk £5.99 0747236712

The Cat Who Moved a Mountain
Headline pbk £5.99 0747239282

The Cat Who Played Brahms
Headline pbk £5.99 0747250367

The Cat Who Played Post Office
Headline pbk £5.99 0747250375

The Cat Who Said Cheese
Headline pbk £5.99 074724944X

The Cat Who Saw Red
Headline pbk £4.99 0747233144

The Cat Who Sniffed Glue
Headline pbk £5.99 074723325X

The Cat Who Talked to Ghosts
Headline pbk £4.99 0747234884

The Cat Who Turned On and Off
Headline pbk £5.99 0747233241

The Cat Who Wasn't There
Headline pbk £5.99 0747241341

The Cat Who Went Into the Closet
Headline pbk £5.99 0747242658

SIMON BRETT

Compiler of successful anthologies, including the *Faber Book of Diaries,* and author of the humorous introduction to the delights of parenthood, *How to Be a Little Sod,* Simon Brett is also a prolific writer of detective stories, many of them featuring the boozy actor/sleuth Charles Paris. The plots are far-fetched but Brett's cynical wit and skilful evocation of the less glamorous side of showbiz make the books very readable. Brett has also written a series of titles involving the intrepid Mrs Pargeter, a sixty-something widow with a gift for attracting rather more murder and mystery than does the average pensioner.

Dead Romantic
Pan pbk £4.99 0330338773

Mrs Pargeter's Package
Pan pbk £4.99 0330317342

Mrs, Presumed Dead
Pan pbk £4.99 0330314890

Murder Unprompted
Gollancz pbk £5.99 0575600209

A Reconstructed Corpse
Gollancz pbk £4.99 0575057815

A Shock to the System
Pan pbk £4.99 0330315951

Sicken and So Die
Gollancz pbk £4.99 0575600489

Singled Out
Pan pbk £4.99 0330344412

Situation Tragedy
Gollancz pbk £4.99 0575600195

CHRISTOPHER BROOKMYRE

Jack Parlabane, in the two novels so far published by Christopher Brookmyre, is a cynical journo who has seen it all and had most of it done to him. In many ways he is the traditional private investigator of a lot of hard-boiled fiction. He drinks too much and has a murky past. He is prepared to commit minor misdemeanours – basic breaking and entering and computer hacking for beginners – in pursuit of greater criminals. Parlabane is saved from cliché by the reality of the political context in which Brookmyre places him and by the specific detail of the Scotland within which he operates. Parlabane is shown as having a particular loathing of the hypocrisies and abuses of political power and, in the two books, goes up against a scheming NHS Trust chief executive and a monstrously corrupt Scottish Secretary of State. *Quite Ugly One Morning* and Brookmyre's second novel, *The Country of the Blind,* are scabrous, witty, violent and welcome additions to the growing list of British crime fiction which tackles the issues of contemporary Britain.

The Country of the Blind
Little Brown pbk £9.99 0316641766

Quite Ugly One Morning
Little Brown pbk £6.99 0349108854

EDWARD BUNKER

Eddie Bunker has lived the life he portrays in his work. His own experience informs every page of his books. Bunker was born in Hollywood in 1933 to alcoholic, dysfunctional parents. Deprived of a stable family environment, he progressed from foster homes to boarding schools to military schools and eventually to Juvenile Hall. It was there that the young Bunker first mixed with the hardened criminals who educated him in the life he was to lead in the decades to come. For twenty years he was involved in drug deals, robberies, extortion and forgery and made it to the FBI's Ten Most Wanted list. Inevitably he spent much time in brutal prisons and it was in prison that he began to write, inspired, he claims, by the sound of Caryl Chessman's typewriter clacking on Death Row. His first novel, published in 1973, was *No Beast So Fierce*, an explosive, no-holds-barred narrative which is both exciting and repellent. In subsequent novels, *The Animal Factory* and *Little Boy Blue*, Bunker again fictionalised his own experiences to illustrate the violent, corrupting influences of institutional life and the difficulties of ex-cons going straight in a society that excludes them. Through his work Bunker has overcome those difficulties and has divided his time between writing and acting, most famously as Mr Blue in *Reservoir Dogs*. In his recent novel, *Dog Eat Dog*, his first for fifteen years, he draws once again on his own life and on stories heard in prison to produce a highly paced, tense thriller that is also an examination of friendship and loyalty and society's attitude to its outcasts and criminals.

The Animal Factory
No Exit Press pbk £5.99 1874061270

Dog Eat Dog
No Exit Press pbk £5.99 1874061505

Little Boy Blue
No Exit Press pbk £5.99 1874061262

No Beast So Fierce
No Exit Press pbk £5.99 1874061092

JAMES LEE BURKE

James Lee Burke is one of the most evocative and atmospheric of contemporary American crime writers, rooted in a strong sense of place and, together with such novelists as James Ellroy and James Crumley, someone who has made the traditional differentiation between genre writing and 'literary' writing seem increasingly irrelevant. His reputation has been established by his series of nine books featuring Cajun detective Dave Robicheaux. Robicheaux is one of the most complex and satisfying heroes in crime fiction and the New Orleans and Louisiana in which he operates are richly and vividly recreated. No-one has captured the city and its particular spirit as well as Burke. He is an intricate plotter whose narrative gifts and ability to describe action and violence are second to none but the greatest strengths of his books lie in the distinctive, poetic prose in which he expresses his vision of crime and redemption, love and despair.

Black Cherry Blues
Arrow pbk £6.99 0099721406
Burning Angel
Phoenix pbk £5.99 1857994078
Cadillac Jukebox
Phoenix pbk £5.99 0752809628
Cimarron Rose
Orion hbk £16.99 0752804863
Dixie City Jam
Phoenix pbk £5.99 1857992466
Half of Paradise
Phoenix pbk £5.99 1857998545
Heaven's Prisoners
Vintage pbk £5.99 009968960X
In the Electric Mist with Confederate Dead
Phoenix pbk £6.99 1857994949
The James Lee Burke Trilogy
Picador pbk £9.99 0330321188
A Morning for Flamingos
Arrow pbk £6.99 0099867109
The Neon Rain
Vintage pbk £5.99 0099689707
A Stained White Radiance
Arrow pbk £6.99 0099144913

W. J. BURLEY

The books featuring the dogged Cornish detective, Chief Superintendent Wycliffe, have been given a boost by the TV series starring Jack Shepherd. Burley has been publishing detective fiction since the 1960s and his novels, with their sense of place and setting in the West Country, are skilfully and professionally written.

Wycliffe and Death in a Salubrious Place
Corgi pbk £3.99 055214116X
Wycliffe and Death in Stanley Street
Corgi pbk £4.99 0552136891
Wycliffe and How to Kill a Cat
Corgi pbk £3.99 0552141178
Wycliffe and the Beales
Corgi pbk £4.99 0552132322
Wycliffe and the Cycle of Death
Corgi pbk £4.99 0552141097
Wycliffe and the Dead Flautist
Corgi pbk £3.99 0552142646
Wycliffe and the Dunes Mystery
Corgi pbk £4.99 0552142212

Wycliffe and the Four Jacks
Corgi pbk £4.99 0552142670
Wycliffe and the Guilt-Edged Alibi
Corgi pbk £4.99 0552141151
Wycliffe and the House of Fear
Corgi pbk £4.99 0552144371
Wycliffe and the Last Rites
Corgi pbk £4.99 0552142654
Wycliffe and the Pea-Green Boat
Corgi pbk £4.99 055212804X
Wycliffe and the Quiet Virgin
Corgi pbk £4.99 055213435X
Wycliffe and the Scapegoat
Corgi pbk £4.99 0552142662

Wycliffe and the Tangled Web
Corgi pbk £4.99 0552142689
Wycliffe and the Three-Toed Pussy
Corgi pbk £4.99 0552142050
Wycliffe and the Winsor Blue
Corgi pbk £4.99 0552134368
Wycliffe in Paul's Court
Corgi pbk £4.99 0552134333
Wycliffe and the Wild-Goose Chase
Corgi pbk £4.99 0552142697

W. R. BURNETT (1899–1982)

Burnett was a pioneer of the gangster novel and his book *Little Caesar*, published in 1929, was a model for many of the pulp writers of the thirties and forties. *Little Caesar* was made into a memorable film starring Edward G.Robinson and Burnett's later novel, *The Asphalt Jungle*, which appeared in 1949, was filmed by John Huston. Burnett was a prolific author of fiction about prizefighters and professional sportsmen, jazz musicians and the mythical heroes of the American West, but it is as a chronicler of gangsterism and corrupt politicians that he is best remembered.

The work of W. R. Burnett is not currently available in this country but American editions of his books may be available in some larger branches of Waterstone's.

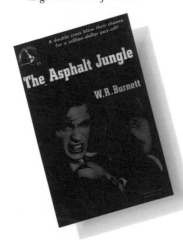

JAMES M. CAIN (1892–1977)

A critic described James M. Cain as the 'poet of the tabloid murder'. His stories invite us to pry into the lustful, obsessive lives of his characters and perhaps find something of our selves there. Cain was born in Maryland in 1892 and received a college education. He trained as an opera singer, then worked at a variety of jobs before becoming a successful journalist, rising to become managing editor of *The New Yorker*. He moved to Hollywood in the early 30s to write screenplays but he was not notably successful and turned to fiction to support himself. His first novel *The Postman Always Rings Twice* appeared in 1934 and was a huge success, selling over a million copies. Cain's reputation is founded on this book and a handful of other novels written in the 30s and 40s – *Double Indemnity, Serenade, The Butterfly* and *Mildred Pierce*. Although he continued to write until his death in 1977, his later works, mainly on historical themes, are little read today. Tersely written, explicit (for the period) in their depiction of sex and violence, Cain's crime stories are low-rent tragedies of obsession among ordinary people. They achieve their voyeuristic power through the device of first person confessional storytelling. These crimes are not reported from the detective's point of view – 'the least interesting angle', Cain called it – but from that of the criminal. This means Cain can take an amoral, non-judgemental attitude to the action. Unprotected by looking through the 'safety-glass' of a private eye, the reader is further involved in the story. The novels invariably end with the criminal revealing that the story is a confession – written on death row in the case of *The Postman Always Rings Twice*. These characters are helpless before their fate once they have set their stories in motion; there is no room for the questioning and doubt found in the detective story.

Five Great Novels of James M. Cain
Picador pbk £8.99 0330291130

ROBERT CAMPBELL

Robert Campbell is the author of over twenty crime novels, including *The Junkyard Dog* which won an Edgar Award and *In La-La Land We Trust* which was chosen by the *Washington Post* as the best crime novel of 1986. He has also written various television plays and screenplays, including the Oscar-nominated *The Man of a Thousand Faces*. His two main series characters, Jimmy Flannery and Whistler ('he had a first name but with a last name like Whistler, hardly anybody ever used it') live and work in different cities and inhabit, it sometimes seems, different universes. Flannery is a volunteer worker for the Democratic Party in Chicago and his world revolves around politics. The stories are well-plotted, the dialogue catchy and the humour light. Whistler's world is much darker. He works in Los Angeles – Hollywood (La-La Land) to be more precise – and is a failed actor turned private eye. He lives surrounded by pimps, whores, transvestites, paedophiles, celebrities and crooked cops. A few have hearts of gold but most are twisted, amoral and greedy. The two series have little in common beyond Campbell's surefooted storytelling but serve to indicate the versatility of one of America's best contemporary crime writers.

Robert Campbell's work is currently out of print in the UK. Imports of American editions may be available in some larger branches of Waterstone's.

JOHN LE CARRE

Le Carré is, of course, renowned for his fiction of the Cold War and as the writer who, more than any other, raised the spy thriller to its highest standards with his complexly plotted and morally ambiguous novels. His first two books, both featuring an earlier version of his famous character George Smiley, were written when Le Carré was himself still at the Foreign Office and therefore published under the pseudonym which has become so well known. They are nearer detective fiction than spy thrillers, in which Smiley investigates the murders of a schoolmaster's wife, in *Murder of Quality* and a Foreign Office official, in *Call for the Dead*, and they are usually classified as such.

Call for the Dead
Hodder pbk £5.99 0340559691
Murder of Quality
Hodder pbk £5.99 0340554444

RAYMOND CHANDLER (1888–1959)

For many people Philip Marlowe is the epitome of the private
detective, a loner walking the rainswept streets in trenchcoat
and hat, wisecracking and taking a beating before going home
to an empty room to find meaning in the bottom of a bottle. All
private eyes, whether in novels or on radio, TV or cinema draw
on the mythic figure of Marlowe, created by Chandler. Marlowe
inhabits a Southern California of dusty offices and ritzy night
clubs, of fake diamonds on people with quick money or no
money, a place as unstable as a cheap apartment block in the
earthquake zone. His heart is his sense of honour. He alone can
travel through the corruption and remain uncorrupted. 'Down
these mean streets a man must go who is not himself mean,
who is neither tarnished nor afraid,' as Chandler wrote.
Marlowe becomes more world-weary and cynical with each story
– try *The Long Goodbye* for bitterness and betrayal – because,
unlike the classic English detective, he knows that finally he
cannot win. Miss Marple will solve the murder in the country-
house garden and the world will be tidy again - but Marlowe's
LA will still be a place where 'Twenty-four hours a day somebody is running, somebody else is trying to catch him . . . a city
lost and beaten and full of emptiness.' (The Long Goodbye)
Chandler's own life seems to reflect the character of Marlowe,
his sense of being a man out of place and out of time. Although
born in the USA in 1888 he moved to England as a boy and
attended Dulwich College, a public school, from 1900 to 1904,
absorbing the ethos of the English middle classes. After school
he tried to earn a living in England from writing poetry and
reviews before war service in France was followed by a period of
drifting from job to job in the USA. Eventually he settled in the
oil industry in LA where he made and then lost a fortune. In

1933, out of work and short of money, Chandler returned to writing, choosing to try the detective genre. He worked slowly, even painfully, to produce about twenty stories for pulp magazines such as *Black Mask* and *Dime Detective* between 1933 and 1941. Some of these were recycled later to provide material for the novels. From 1939 Chandler turned to writing full-length novels, publishing seven in all, from *The Big Sleep* in 1939 to *Playback* in 1958. He continued to find writing difficult and work was interrupted by bouts of ill-health, depression and alcoholism. He died in 1959. Chandler also worked in Hollywood, 'the Golden Graveyard', as he called it, in the 1940s. He worked on several screenplays, most notably for Billy Wilder's *Double Indemnity*, taken from James M. Cain's novel. A number of films have been made from his own stories – our image of Marlowe is hard to separate from Bogart's portrayal of him in Howard Hawks's 1946 film *The Big Sleep*. The Marlowe novels were among the first detective stories to emphasise character and atmosphere rather than plot. Indeed Chandler can sometimes seem only perfunctorily interested in his plots – there is, for example, a wholly unexplained murder in *The Big Sleep*. At their best – *The Long Goodbye, Farewell, My Lovely, The Big Sleep* – the books are superbly written, making full use of the much-imitated wisecracks and unlikely similes. They are filled with passages of evocative description and are possessed of a coherent sense of place and a philosophy which are closely integrated into the stories. Chandler's work moves beyond the limits of the genre to explore wider themes. His books are not just detective stories but significant works of American literature.

The Big Sleep
Penguin pbk £6.99 0140108920

Farewell My Lovely
Penguin pbk £6.99 014010979X

The High Window
Penguin pbk £6.99 0140108939

Killer in the Rain
Penguin pbk £6.99 0140109005

The Lady in the Lake
Penguin pbk £6.99 0140108947

The Little Sister
Penguin pbk £6.99 0140108963

The Long Goodbye
Penguin pbk £6.99 0140108955

Pearls Are a Nuisance
Penguin pbk £6.99 0140108998

Playback
Penguin pbk £6.99 0140108971

Smart Alec Kill
Penguin pbk £6.99 014010898X

Trouble is My Business
Penguin pbk £6.99 0140109803

'It was a blonde. A blonde to make a bishop kick a hole in a stained-glass window.'

Raymond Chandler

JEROME CHARYN

Charyn had already written seven novels before embarking on his first detective story and he only wrote that, in an act of desperation, because he was stuck halfway through his eighth. Charyn is a writer of exceptionally vivid prose. His first four crime novels - more accurately, novellas – link up to form *The Isaac Quartet*, written in the seventies, but not collected in one volume until 1984. The quartet was extended later by the publication of *The Good Policeman*. These books are certainly an acquired taste, with their wild characterisation and surreal sense of the New York in which the protagonist, Isaac Sidel, operates as mainman of the First Deputy Police Commissioner's Office, but they are fascinating works for anyone who likes to see the boundaries of crime fiction extended. Sadly the earlier books are currently out of print in the UK. The only book available which gives some sense of Charyn's idiosyncratic but rewarding approach to genre fiction is Maria's Girls, published by Serpent's Tail.

Maria's Girls
Serpent's Tail pbk £7.99 1852421541

KATE CHARLES

Kate Charles describes visiting churches as her favourite pastime, which is appropriate for the author of a series of clerical mysteries featuring her hero David Middleton-Brown. Once dubbed by a writer in the Guardian 'a bloodstained version of Barbara Pym', she is adept at the construction of lively stories of malicious gossip, petty thievery, blackmail and worse among the less virtuous members of the church.

Appointed to Die
Headline pbk £4.99 0747241996

A Dead Man Out of Mind
Headline pbk £5.99 0747245355

A Drink of Deadly Wine
Headline pbk £5.99 0747237670

Evil Angels Among Them
Headline pbk £5.99 074725219X

The Snares of Death
Headline pbk £5.99 0747238731

G. K. CHESTERTON (1874–1936)

Chesterton's writings were voluminous and ranged from nonsense verse to studies of Dickens and George Bernard Shaw, from religious and political polemic to novels of whimsy and fantasy such as *The Napoleon of Notting Hill* and *The Man Who Was Thursday*. He is probably best remembered today for the stories about the unassuming Catholic priest Father Brown. Chesterton's gift for paradox is revealed in the ingenuity of the puzzles and their solutions in the best of the stories, and the character of Father Brown, forever alert to the frailties of human nature, is a memorable one.

Complete Father Brown
Penguin pbk £9.99 014009766X

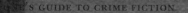

AGATHA CHRISTIE (1890–1976)

The most distinguished and best-known author of the classic
mystery novel was born in Torquay in 1890 and received a conventional middle-class upbringing and education. During the
First World War she worked in a hospital dispensary and it was
here, surrounded by poisons and encouraged by her elder sister, that she wrote her first detective novel. This was published
in 1920 as *The Mysterious Affair at Styles* and introduced the
Belgian detective Hercule Poirot. With his passion for order
and method, Poirot quickly established himself in the imagination of the public, using his 'little grey cells' to solve the most
intricate and complex crimes. It is in the Poirot novels that
Christie's writing is at its most fluent; the books are impeccably
clued and the solutions are ingenious.

In her private life Agatha Christie was always extremely shy
and shunned publicity to an almost obsessional degree. It was
this introverted self-absorption, compounded by her marital
breakdown, that led to a real-life mystery as intriguing as anything that appeared in her eighty four novels. In 1926 she disappeared for several days. Her car was found abandoned and
the police undertook a nationwide search, inflamed by a fren-

zied media which suspected foul play. She was eventually traced to a hotel in Harrogate where she appeared to be suffering from amnesia. Unlike the mysteries she wrote, her disappearance has never been successfully explained.

If after this incident Christie hoped to retire from the public gaze, Hercule Poirot prevented her. Her readers' love of this character, and her own need for financial independence, led her to the most successful period of her career, in which she produced a series of intricately plotted, compelling mysteries, including *Murder on the Orient Express*, *The ABC Murders*, *Death on the Nile* and the seminal *The Murder of Roger Ackroyd* which, with its truly shocking denouement, remains a classic of the genre.

As if spurning the ostentations of Poirot, Christie created another detective, the antithesis of the Belgian sleuth. Miss Jane Marple, the elderly spinster with astonishing powers of deduction, made her first appearance in *The Murder at the Vicarage* in 1930. This deceptively mild old lady (based partly on Christie's

own grandmother) uses her profound knowledge of human nature, gleaned from a lifetime spent observing the inhabitants of her village St. Mary Mead, in order to solve a series of unusual and perplexing cases. Lacking the flamboyant eccentricities of Poirot, Miss Marple is a subtler, arguably more successful character study and Christie herself often expressed great fondness for her. The novels in which Miss Marple is best seen include *A Murder is Announced*, *The Body in the Library*, *The 4.50 from Paddington* and *The Moving Finger.*

Christie's output was prodigious. As well as the Poirot and Marple novels, she wrote a lesser series featuring 'bright young things' and amateur detectives Tommy and Tuppence Beresford, and many non-series books and collections of short stories. She also wrote plays, including *The Mousetrap*, the longest running play in history, and, under the pseudonym of Mary Westmacott, she produced a number of romances.

Although her style is often undistinguished and her characterization sometimes unconvincing, particularly in her later novels, Agatha Christie's mastery of the crime narrative is beyond doubt. Her ingenuity in constructing complex plots and her skill at deceiving readers and sustaining suspense go a long way towards explaining her supremacy as a crime novelist and her enduring popularity. In addition to her command of the genre's strategies of deception, her books are filled with the period detail which effortlessly evokes a vanished world of English villages, country hotels, steam railways and ocean liners. The fictional world in which her webs of deception, adultery and murder are spun is one that is both recognisable and romanticised and perhaps this explains her abiding popularity.

4.50 From Paddington
HarperCollins pbk £3.99
0006157629

The ABC Murders
HarperCollins pbk £4.99
0006498728

Absent in the Spring
HarperCollins pbk £4.99
0006499473

The Adventure of the Christmas Pudding
HarperCollins pbk £3.99
0006168175

After the Funeral
HarperCollins pbk £3.99
0006162754

And Then There Were None
HarperCollins pbk £3.99
0006165400

Appointment With Death
HarperCollins pbk £3.99
0006140459

At Bertram's Hotel
HarperCollins pbk £3.99
0006169228

The Big Four
HarperCollins pbk £3.99
000616918X

The Body in the Library
HarperCollins pbk £4.99
0006167497

The Burden
HarperCollins pbk £4.99
0006499503

By the Pricking of My Thumbs
HarperCollins pbk £3.99
0006165702

Cards on the Table
HarperCollins pbk £4.99
0006498736

A Caribbean Tale
HarperCollins pbk £3.99
0006164358

Cat Among the Pigeons
HarperCollins pbk £4.99
000616174X

The Clocks
HarperCollins pbk £3.99
0006161731

Crooked House
HarperCollins pbk £3.99
0006168647

Curtain: Poirot's Last Case
HarperCollins pbk £3.99
0006168000

A Daughter's A Daughter
HarperCollins pbk £3.99
00064949X

Dead Man's Folly
HarperCollins pbk £3.99
0006168035

Death Comes as the End
HarperCollins pbk £4.99
0006163734

Death in the Clouds
HarperCollins pbk £3.99
0006169260

Death on the Nile
HarperCollins pbk £5.99
0006499678

Destination Unknown
HarperCollins pbk £3.99
0006169163

Dumb Witness
HarperCollins pbk £4.99
0006168086

Elephants Can Remember
HarperCollins pbk £3.99
0006162649

Endless Night
HarperCollins pbk £3.99
000616823X

Evil Under the Sun
HarperCollins pbk £3.99
0006170048

Five Little Pigs
HarperCollins pbk £3.99
0006163726

Giant's Bread
HarperCollins pbk £4.99
0006499457

Hallowe'en Party
HarperCollins pbk £4.99
0006161723

Hercule Poirot's Christmas
HarperCollins pbk £3.99
0006169325

Hickory Dickory Dock
HarperCollins pbk £3.99
0006170005

The Hollow
HarperCollins pbk £4.99
0006165516

The Hound of Death and Other Stories
HarperCollins pbk £3.99
0006171044

The Labours of Hercules
HarperCollins pbk £3.99
0006171184

The Listerdale Mystery
HarperCollins pbk £3.99
0006167365

Lord Edgware Dies
HarperCollins pbk £4.99
0006165397

The Man in the Brown Suit
HarperCollins pbk £4.99
0006174752

The Mirror Crack'd from Side to Side
HarperCollins pbk £3.99
0006169309

Miss Marple Omnibus Vol 1
HarperCollins pbk £8.99
0006499597

Miss Marple Omnibus Vol 2
HarperCollins pbk £8.99
0006499600

Miss Marple Omnibus Vol 3
HarperCollins pbk £8.99
0006499619

Miss Marple: Complete Short Stories
HarperCollins pbk £6.99
0006499627

Miss Marple's Final Cases
HarperCollins pbk £4.99
0006167950

The Moving Finger
HarperCollins pbk £3.99
0006172695

Mrs McGinty's Dead
HarperCollins pbk £3.99
0006163718

The Murder at the Vicarage
HarperCollins pbk £3.99
0006161308

Murder in Mesopotamia
HarperCollins pbk £3.99
0006170706

Murder in the Mews
HarperCollins pbk £4.99
0006167144

A Murder Is Announced
HarperCollins pbk £4.99
0006165281

Murder Is Easy
HarperCollins pbk £4.99
0006168132

The Murder of Roger Ackroyd
HarperCollins pbk £3.99
0006167926

The Murder on the Links
HarperCollins pbk £3.99
0006174779

Murder on the Orient Express
HarperCollins pbk £3.99
0006170064

The Mysterious Affair at Styles
HarperCollins pbk £3.99
0006174744

The Mysterious Mr Quin
HarperCollins pbk £3.99
0006166512

The Mystery of the Blue Train
HarperCollins pbk £3.99
0006170765

N or M?
HarperCollins pbk £4.99
0006163017

Nemesis
HarperCollins pbk £3.99
0006170056

One, Two, Buckle My Shoe
HarperCollins pbk £3.99
0006166911

Ordeal by Innocence
HarperCollins pbk £3.99
0006170676

The Pale Horse
HarperCollins pbk £3.99
0006164382

Parker Pyne Investigates
HarperCollins pbk £3.99
0006164773

Partners in Crime
HarperCollins pbk £3.99
0006171168

Passenger to Frankfurt
HarperCollins pbk £3.99
0006164498

Peril at End House
HarperCollins pbk £3.99
000616613X

A Pocket Full of Rye
HarperCollins pbk £3.99
0006168914

Poirot Investigates
HarperCollins pbk £3.99
0006174795

Poirot's Early Cases
HarperCollins pbk £3.99
0006167128

Postern of Fate
HarperCollins pbk £3.99
0006165273

Problem at Pollensa Bay
HarperCollins pbk £3.99
0006472427

The Rose and the Yew Tree
HarperCollins pbk £4.99
0006499481

Sad Cypress
HarperCollins pbk £3.99
0006167209

The Secret Adversary
HarperCollins pbk £3.99
0006174787

The Secret of Chimneys
HarperCollins pbk £3.99
0006174760

The Seven Dials Mystery
HarperCollins pbk £3.99
0006165419

The Sittaford Mystery
HarperCollins pbk £3.99
0006168167

Sleeping Murder
HarperCollins pbk £3.99
0006165338

Sparkling Cyanide
HarperCollins pbk £3.99
0006162630

Taken at the Flood
HarperCollins pbk £3.99
0006168892

They Came to Baghdad
HarperCollins pbk £3.99
0006166059

They Do It With Mirrors
HarperCollins pbk £3.99
0006165591

Third Girl
HarperCollins pbk £4.99
0006172636

The Thirteen Problems
HarperCollins pbk £3.99
0006162746

Three Act Tragedy
HarperCollins pbk £4.99
0006154174

Towards Zero
HarperCollins pbk £3.99
0006163858

Dead Man's Folly
HarperCollins pbk £3.99
0006168035

Unfinished Portrait
HarperCollins pbk £4.99
0006499465

While the Light Lasts
HarperCollins hbk £14.99
0002326434

Agatha Christie wrote stories for a number of magazines in the twenties and thirties and most of these found their way into the collections published in her life-time. The eight stories in this volume, published in 1997, have not previously been collected and have not been published since their first appearance in the twenties.

MICHAEL CLYNES

One of the best historical mystery writers around is P. C. Doherty. He is also one of the most prolific. Under the pseudonym of Michael Clynes he has published a sequence of books about the reprobate Sir Roger Shallot, a kind of Tudor Flashman, who operates amidst both the splendours of Henry VIII's court and the more fetid alleyways of sixteenth century London.

A Brood of Vipers
Headline pbk £5.99 0747244758

The Gallows Murders
Headline pbk £5.99 0747249288

The Grail Murders
Headline pbk £4.99 0747242631

The Poisoned Chalice
Headline pbk £4.99 0747239657

The Relic Murders
Headline pbk £5.99 0747254400

The White Rose Murders
Headline pbk £5.99 0747237859

LIZA CODY

Liza Cody once funded her writing by a job at Madame Tussaud's, making the fingers for the waxworks. An unusual job for someone who has created two of the most unusual heroines in modern British crime fiction. Eva Wylie is a female wrestler, barred from the ring, who turns detective in her spare time. For Eva crime-fighting often leads to other kinds of fighting and she numbers her two rottweiler crossbreeds amongst her closest friends. Anna Lee is a dissatisfied private investigator with a security firm who has to deal with her disapproving boss's preoccupation with paperwork and her own disturbing capacity for attracting trouble while investigating what seem to be the simplest of cases. Cody's stories of London life and crime are peopled by a variety of colourful characters – from the band of prostitutes to whom Eva teaches her own peculiar brand of self defence to the delightfully odd poet who is Anna's downstairs neighbour – and told with great verve and humour. Her two strong, believable yet fallible central characters are welcome presences in a domain that is too often seen as exclusively male.

Bucket Nut
Bloomsbury pbk £6.99 0747533873

Musclebound
Bloomsbury hbk £14.99 0747533784

'Hercule Poirot tapped his forehead. "These little grey cells. It is up to them – as you say over here."'

Agatha Christie

WILKIE COLLINS (1824–1889)

Collins, a close friend of Dickens, was an extremely successful novelist with the Victorian public and the leading exponent of what came to be known as 'sensation fiction', a school of fiction which took crime and mystery as its subject. *The Woman in White* is a tangled tale, superbly manipulated by Collins, involving madness, despair, discreditable family secrets and a memorable villain in the fat, suave and sinister Italian count, Fosco. *The Moonstone*, which was first published in 1868, has been described as 'the first, the longest and the best of . . . English detective novels'. In a prologue Collins describes how a British Colonel, during the siege of Seringapatam, steals a diamond from a Hindu holy place. He leaves it to his niece but it is stolen from her Yorkshire home on the morning of her eighteenth birthday. Suspicion falls on various potential culprits but, after major twists and turns in the convoluted plot, the real villain is unmasked. *The Moonstone* also includes one of the first detectives in English fiction, the shrewd and melancholy Sergeant Cuff who is largely instrumental in pointing the finger at the guilty party. Other of Collins's many novels contain elements of suspense and mystery but these two books, always cited in surveys of the genre, were significant landmarks in the history of detective fiction.

The Moonstone
Penguin pbk £2.50 0140430148
The Woman in White
Penguin pbk £2.50 0140430962
The Woman in White
Oxford UP pbk £2.50 0192824031

'Did you notice the time? Was it late?'
'Not very. About twelve o'clock, I think.'
'Did you fall asleep?'
'No. I coudn't sleep that night.'
'You were restless?' . . .

Wilkie Collins, *The Moonstone*

MICHAEL CONNELLY

Hieronymus 'Harry' Bosch is an ex-Vietnam tunnel rat now working as a homicide detective in the reviled Hollywood precinct of the LAPD. He has little respect for authority but gets results. Superficially this suggests the worst sort of hackneyed characterisation but, although Michael Connelly's series of books about Bosch do contain a number of 'Harry, you're off the case' scenes, the author is successful in making most of the set-ups seem fresh. Previously a crime reporter, Connelly is adept at the police procedural stuff and his plots are ingenious and well-constructed. Bosch is made into an extremely sympathetic character with a compelling and complex personal history. The authority he defies is mindless, pencil-pushing and wasteful whereas Bosch's motivation is invariably selfless and professional. Connelly is clearly fond of Los Angeles and pays frequent tribute to the city and its literature. Chandler is constantly alluded to, and the entire plot of *The Last Coyote*, in which Bosch attempts to solve the decades-old murder of his mother, is a clear homage to James Ellroy. *The Poet*, Connelly's one departure from the Bosch series to date, is a successful and deviously constructed serial killer story about a crime reporter unsatisfied that his brother's death was the suicide it appears to be.

The Black Echo
Orion pbk £5.99 0752810006

The Black Ice
Orion pbk £5.99 1857974779

The Concrete Blonde
Orion pbk £5.99 1857974787

The Last Coyote
Orion pbk £5.99 1857974795

The Poet
Orion pbk £5.99 0752809261

Trunk Music
Orion hbk £16.99 0752807005

CLARENCE COOPER JR

(1934–1978)
In the course of a deeply troubled life, plagued by addiction and punctuated by spells in prison, the black American writer Clarence Cooper Junior wrote and published six novels. These extraordinary books, some of which have been republished by the enterprising Payback Press, are novels about crime rather than crime fiction, but deserve to find a large readership for their unrelentingly bleak portrayals of life on the meanest of streets, of addicts and hustlers, pimps and prisoners.

Black
Payback Press pbk £6.99
0862416892

The Farm
Payback Press pbk £5.99
0862416000

The Scene
Payback Press pbk £6.99
0862416345

PATRICIA CORNWELL

To Patricia Cornwell the writing of gripping crime fiction is not so much an art as an exact science. The former morgue computer analyst put her clinical experience to good use in creating Kay Scarpetta, Chief Medical Examiner of Virginia and nemesis of many violent killers. In Scarpetta, Cornwell has introduced one of the most absorbing and complex characters in contemporary crime fiction. She is ambitious, resilient and possessed of a restlessly inquisitive mind, yet she also reveals flashes of an endearing vulnerability. She is an intelligent woman in her middle years who has seen the very worst that human nature has to offer, yet she strives to find goodness where it can be found and to seek retribution for the victims of violent crime whom she encounters on their final journey to the city mortuary. Along with her brilliant and gifted niece Lucy and the sulky, streetwise cop Pete Marino, Scarpetta gradually becomes personally entangled in each of her cases. With the relentless attention to detail which is a hallmark of her writing, Cornwell makes the reader live Scarpetta's nightmare and share in her assessment of grisly crime scenes. Yet these stories are not slasher shockers. The dawning realisation of the dark horrors Scarpetta confronts is subtly achieved and, because of this, much more terrifying. Cornwell's writing has an implacable grip as her characters are propelled towards a heart-stopping climax. With the eighth in the Scarpetta series now published, and the police-based novel *Hornet's Nest*, Cornwell has established herself as one of the finest and bestselling crime writers in the world and has done so without resorting to formulaic plotting and characterisation.

All That Remains
Warner pbk £5.99 0751501107

The Body Farm
Warner pbk £5.99 0751512214

Body of Evidence
Warner pbk £5.99 0751505129

Cause of Death
Warner pbk £5.99 0751519170

Cruel and Unusual
Warner pbk £5.99 0751501689

From Potter's Field
Warner pbk £5.99 0751516309

Hornet's Nest
Little Brown hbk £9.99 0316882526

Post-mortem
Warner pbk £5.99 0751504947

Unnatural Exposure
Little Brown pbk £9.99 0316639842

'I saw a white face beyond the rain-streaked glass, a face form-less and inhuman like the faces of misshapen dolls made of nylon hose.'

**Patricia Cornwell,
Post-mortem**

EDMUND CRISPIN (1921–1978)

Edmund Crispin was the pseudonym of Bruce Montgomery, a composer and writer who was a contemporary and friend of both Philip Larkin and Kingsley Amis at Oxford. He wrote a number of ingenious and amusing detective stories featuring Gervase Fen, the Oxford don and amateur investigator who is one of the most distinctive and entertaining characters to emerge from British crime writing since the war. Fen is closer to the Sherlock Holmes type of detective than to the more realistic characters of recent writing but he is much more than a clever pastiche. Dispassionate, dyspeptic and blessed with a waspish sense of humour, he is his own man and one who regards the solving of a crime as a problem to be simplified just as one might dash off the Times crossword or translate a page or two of Ovid. Of the novels Crispin wrote, a couple stand out. The traditional locked room mystery is surpassed by *The Moving Toyshop* in which, as the title suggests, an entire shop disappears overnight. *Frequent Hearses* sees Fen leaving Oxford for London to work as technical advisor on a film based on, of all things, the life of Alexander Pope. Needless to say, murder soon intervenes. All of Crispin's books are whimsical and self-consciously old-fashioned but they are all worth reading. The excursion through Fen country is worth making.

Buried for Pleasure
Penguin pbk £4.99 0140117709

Fen Country
Penguin pbk £5.99 0140088156

Frequent Hearses
Penguin pbk £5.99 0140093559

The Glimpses of the Moon
Penguin pbk £5.99 0140100741

Holy Disorders
Penguin pbk £5.99 0140117725

The Moving Toyshop
Penguin pbk £5.99 0140088172

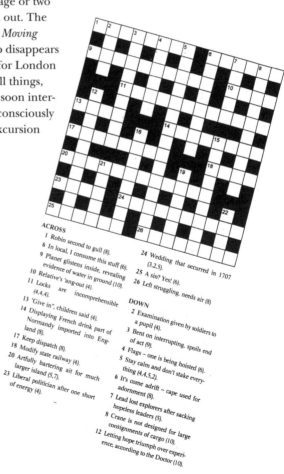

ACROSS

1 Robin second to gull (8).
6 In local, I consume this stuff (6).
9 Planet glistens inside, revealing evidence of water in ground (10).
10 Relative's 'ang-out (4).
11 Locks are incomprehensible (4.4.4).
13 'Give in", children said (4).
14 Displaying French drink part of Normandy imported into England (8).
17 Keep dispatch (8).
18 Modify state railway (4).
20 Artfully bartering ait for much larger island (5,7).
23 Liberal politician after one short of energy (4).
24 Wedding that occurred in 1707 (3,2,5).
25 A sin? Yes! (6).
26 Left struggling, needs air (8)

DOWN

2 Examination given by soldiers to a pupil (4).
3 Bent on interrupting, spoils end of act (9).
4 Flags – one is being hoisted (6).
5 Stay calm and don't stake everything (4,4,5,2).
6 It's come adrift – cape used for adornment (8).
7 Lead lost explorers after sacking hopeless leaders (5).
8 Crane is not designed for large consignments of cargo (10).
12 Letting hope triumph over experience, according to the Doctor (10).

DEBORAH CROMBIE

In the tradition established by Elizabeth George, Deborah Crombie is an American, born in Dallas and now resident in North Texas, who writes well-crafted crime fiction set in England. She has long been an admirer of classic English detective fiction and her novels featuring the Scotland Yard team of Superintendent Duncan Kincaid and Sergeant Gemma James demonstrate how well she has absorbed the lessons of the best of that fiction.

All Shall Be Well
Pan pbk £4.99 0330344137

Leave the Grave Green
Pan pbk £5.99 0330348833

Mourn Not Your Dead
Macmillan hbk £16.99 0333668537

A Share in Death
Pan pbk £4.99 0330342460

AMANDA CROSS

Amanda Cross is the pseudonym of Carolyn Heilbrun, a professor of humanities at Columbia University. Under her real name she has published several works of non-fiction, some of which examine the role of women in literature. She began writing feminist detective stories as Amanda Cross and introduced feisty Kate Fansler. University lecturer Kate is an intelligent, funny and well-read detective, fond of literary quotation and of poking around in the dusty and skeletoned cupboards of academia. Writing with wry humour Cross weaves literature and feminism into the body of her plots. The result is crime fiction which is both stimulating and satisfying.

A Death in the Faculty
Virago pbk £5.99 0860688968

An Imperfect Spy
Virago pbk £6.99 1860490549

In the Last Analysis
Virago pbk £5.99 1853814881

The James Joyce Murder
Virago pbk £5.99 0860680746

No Word From Winifred
Virago pbk £5.99 0860688534

The Players Come Again
Virago pbk £5.99 1853815152

Poetic Justice
Virago pbk £5.99 1853810258

The Question of Max
Virago pbk £5.99 0860681076

Sweet Death, Kind Death
Virago pbk £5.99 0860684830

The Theban Mysteries
Virago pbk £5.99 185381024X

A Trap for Fools
Virago pbk £5.99 1853810932

JAMES CRUMLEY

Crumley's first detective novel, *The Wrong Case,* was published in 1975. His fifth, *Bordersnakes,* was published in Britain in the autumn of 1997, having appeared in the US a year before. Despite this meagre output Crumley has always been a cult favourite – almost universally admired by critics and other writers. Crumley is a great admirer of Chandler – his second novel *The Last Good Kiss* has a Chandleresque title and *The Mexican Tree Duck* begins with a quote from *The High Window* – and he is less interested in the crime novel as whodunnit than as a vehicle for exploring character, landscape and language. His works are investigations of the mythology of the American West, of the freedom of the individual implicit in its wide-open spaces and of the effects of late twentieth century wars on the American individualist, as much as investigations of crimes. Thus Vietnam is a defining experience for C. W. Sughrue, narrator of *The Last Good Kiss* and *The Mexican Tree Duck* and co-star of *Bordersnakes.* Korea performs the same function for Milo Milodragovitch, narrator of *The Wrong Case* and *Dancing Bear* and the other protagonist of *Bordersnakes.* Gunfights and firefights occur every few pages in these books and enough alcohol and recreational drugs are consumed to keep a small township permanently comatose. Male friendships are forged through violence and drink. The villains of the books are the rich and powerful – bankers, lawyers, developers, drugs dealers. Expletives are not deleted and these books are not for the faint-hearted but they do contain some of the crime genre's finest writing on the landscapes of America and on masculinity.

Bordersnakes
HarperCollins hbk £15.99 0002326442

The James Crumley Collection
The Wrong Case, The Last Good Kiss, Dancing Bear
Picador pbk £9.99 0330326155

The Mexican Tree Duck
Picador pbk £5.99 0330335758

LIONEL DAVIDSON

Although much of his work could be defined as thriller writing rather than crime fiction, Lionel Davidson is the only writer, apart from Ruth Rendell under her own name and her pseudonym Barbara Vine, to win the CWA Gold Dagger Award for Best Crime Novel of the year on three occasions. He won his first Gold Dagger for his first book, *The Night of Wenceslas*, published in 1960, in which a Westerner in Prague is drawn into the shady world of east European politics. After winning again in 1966, with *A Long Way to Shiloh*, Davidson scored a third triumph in 1978 with a tale of gruesome killings in London, *The Chelsea Murders*. Davidson published nothing for a long period of time after *The Chelsea Murders* but recently demonstrated that he is still a powerful force in crime and thriller writing with his 1994 book *Kolymsky Heights*.

Kolymsky Heights
Mandarin pbk £5.99 0749317132

A Long Way to Shiloh
Mandarin pbk £5.99 0749317183

Making Good Again
Mandarin pbk £5.99 0749317140

The Night of Wenceslas
Mandarin pbk £5.99 0749317124

The Rose of Tibet
Mandarin pbk £5.99 0749317167

Smith's Gazelle
Mandarin pbk £5.99 0749317191

The Sun Chemist
Mandarin pbk £5.99 0749317159

LINDSEY DAVIS

Lindsey Davis, in her much-praised series of novels, shares her enthusiasm for the history of Ancient Rome and brings it to life with a racy narrative style and a tongue in cheek wit that don't preclude scholarly accuracy. From the first novel, *The Silver Pigs*, the tone is set. Marcus Didius Falco, memorably described by one critic as 'Philip Marlowe in Ancient Rome', departs the city to track down a scam taking place in the furthest flung and most godforsaken corner of the Empire - Britain. He narrowly avoids a sticky end far from civilization and forms an unlikely partnership with Helena Justina, an aristocratic Roman lady with attitude. On his return to Rome he becomes an Imperial agent to Vespasian. In the novels that follow Falco, often in company with his friend Petronius, a captain of the Aventine watch, takes a tour of everything that is corrupt and nasty in Rome and in the more exotic parts of the Empire. Still involved with the feisty Helena Justina he strives to rise above his plebeian roots and his often disreputable family in order to become an acceptable suitor for a senator's daughter. Everyone from Vespasian and his sons to the criminal lowlife of the city appears to be in a conspiracy to keep him where he is. These hugely enjoyable books constitute some of the best historical crime fiction available.

A Dying Light in Corduba
Arrow pbk £5.99 0099338912

The Iron Hand of Mars
Arrow pbk £5.99 0099200910

Last Act in Palmyra
Arrow pbk £5.99 0099831805

Poseidon's Gold
Arrow pbk £5.99 0099831902

Shadows in Bronze
Pan pbk £5.99 0330311840

The Silver Pigs
Pan pbk £5.99 0330311832

Three Hands in the Fountain
Hutchinson hbk £15.99
0712677917

Time to Depart
Arrow pbk £5.99 0099338815

Venus in Copper
Arrow pbk £5.99 0099831708

COLIN DEXTER

Effortlessly erudite (the quotations that start every chapter are a joy in themselves), the work of Colin Dexter is known to millions through the television adaptations of his books featuring Chief Inspector Morse. A heavy drinker and miserly, on the page the character of Morse is more gritty and less sympathetic than John Thaw's portrayal. The relationship between himself and Sergeant Lewis is the classic crime partnership of investigative genius and diligent sidekick, that is saved from cliché by the framework of police procedure that falls on Lewis' shoulders. (Interestingly enough the character of Lewis has changed in the latest books from the early ones to fit the casting in the television series.) Oxford is the third constant in Dexter's work, the 'dreaming spires' of the city and more importantly the University are an ever-present backdrop to the crimes that Morse investigates and solves. The latest book in the series also clears one of the enigmas surrounding Morse – his Christian name.

The Daughters of Cain
Pan pbk £4.99 0330341634

The Dead of Jericho
Pan pbk £4.99 0330266934

Death Is Now My Neighbour
Pan pbk £5.99 033035034X

The First Inspector Morse Omnibus
Pan pbk £7.99 0330335588

The Jewel That Was Ours
Pan pbk £5.99 0330324195

Last Bus to Woodstock
Pan pbk £4.99 0330248960

Last Seen Wearing
Pan pbk £4.99 0330251481

Morse's Greatest Mystery
Pan pbk £4.99 0330340255

The Riddle of the Third Mile
Pan pbk £4.99 0330283928

The Second Inspector Morse
Omnibus Pan pbk £7.99 0330335596

The Secret of Annexe 3
Pan pbk £4.99 033029976X

Service of All the Dead
Pan pbk £4.99 0330261487

The Silent World of Nicholas Quinn
Pan pbk £4.99 0330254243

The Third Inspector Morse Omnibus
Pan pbk £7.99 033033560X

The Way Through the Woods
Pan pbk £5.99 0330328387

The Wench is Dead
Pan pbk £4.99 0330313363

DELACORTA

Writing in French, Swiss critic Daniel Odier produced a series of witty and outrageous homages to American crime, published under the pseudonym of Delacorta. These chronicle the escapades of genteel criminal mastermind Serge Gorodish, a middle-aged aesthete who, accompanied by the kinky nymphet thief Alba, commits crime for art's sake. The first, most accomplished and only Gorodish novel currently available is *Diva*, which Jean-Jacques Beineix made into a highly successful film in 1982. A young postman comes into possession of a bootleg tape of a performance by a capricious opera singer, who has always refused to make any recordings for fear of compromising her art. Gangsters are in pursuit of the tape and Gorodish enters the fray in his own stylish fashion. Although European in execution, *Diva* shows respect for the virtues of American crime writing – economy of prose, virtuoso plotting and quirky but convincing characterisation. For all its surface sheen it is a substantial work of crime fiction.

Diva
Bloomsbury pbk £5.99 074753182X

MICHAEL DIBDIN

Michael Dibdin's earliest novels, including one in which the Victorian poet Robert Browning acted as amateur detective, were poised delicately between pastiche and authenticity. His Aurelio Zen novels, for which he is now best known, are written with an affection for the varied political and geographical landscapes of Italy, which he knows well. Dibdin uses his knowledge of the country and of its labyrinthine bureaucracy to construct plots which are notable for their constant capacity to surprise the reader. Zen's position as an investigator for the Ministry of the Interior often means that he has to juggle the search for an answer with the need to keep his job beyond the next governmental shake up. Indeed the reports Zen files at the end of his investigations often bear only a passing resemblance to the truth he has unearthed. In *Cabal*, for instance, Zen is brought in to confirm a verdict of suicide where murder would be convenient to no-one. Only when events put his reputation of clever fixer at risk is he forced to reconsider the case and his own position as law keeper or breaker.

Dibdin has continued to alternate his Zen books with other novels in which he takes delight in manipulating the conventions of crime fiction. In *Dirty Tricks* the nameless narrator, in trying to prove his innocence of murder, confesses to a catalogue of despicable deeds. Dibdin plays with the readers' sympathies by asking us to consider not whether or not the anti-hero is guilty but whether or not we want him to get away with the sins he has wittily confessed. All of Dibdin's books, Zen and non-Zen, are cleverly constructed and intriguing mysteries and, as a keen observer and cataloguer of the blurring of wrong and not-so-wrong in contemporary society, he has achieved his position as a challenging and original storyteller.

INSPECTOR ZEN NOVELS

Cabal
Faber pbk £5.99 0571168337

Cosi Fan Tutti
Faber pbk £5.99 0571090561

Dead Lagoon
Faber pbk £5.99 0571173470

Ratking
Faber pbk £5.99 0571154212

Vendetta
Faber pbk £5.99 0571161650

OTHERS

Dark Spectre
Faber pbk £5.99 0571177530

Dirty Tricks
Faber pbk £5.99 0571165303

The Dying of the Light
Faber pbk £4.99 0571170285

The Last Sherlock Holmes Story
Faber pbk £5.99 0571140785

A Rich Full Death
Faber pbk £5.99 0571150454

The Tryst
Faber pbk £5.99 0571142214

'All the elements of the case were now fitting them together in the right way, deciphered.' Michael Dibdin, *Dead Lagoon*

STEPHEN DOBYNS

A chronically underrated writer, Dobyns is also a poet and author of several excellent non-crime novels. His main contribution to detective fiction is as the creator of the Saratoga novels, an admirable series featuring the ex-police officer and now private eye Charlie Bradshaw. Mostly set in Saratoga, the racing town in upstate New York, the books are fine portrayals of small town life with splashes of local colour and generous helpings of humour. Charlie Bradshaw is a superb character – genial and possessed of a nice line in self-deprecatory wit, he's also a determined and persistent investigator. A policeman for twenty years, who quit the force because of an investigation that turned sour, Charlie still tangles with the Saratoga police chief Peterson, another in crime fiction's long line of officious and incompetent officers of the law. Three of the Saratoga books are available in one volume as *Saratoga Trifecta* which serves as a fine introduction to the series and to Charlie Bradshaw. Dobyns's most recent book is a non-Saratoga novel and, although set in a small East coast town, bears no resemblance to the Bradshaw books. *The Church of Dead Girls* is a brilliant study of paranoia and repressed desires in which, one by one, three teenage girls are abducted. As each successive abduction rocks the small community, Dobyns strips away the picture postcard facade to reveal hidden fears and unspoken prejudices. Building to a shattering climax which lingers in the mind long after the reader has put the book down, this is a deeply unsettling work by a major American writer.

The Church of Dead Girls
Penguin pbk £9.99 0670877425

Saratoga Trifecta
Penguin pbk £8.99 0140251960

before him. It was just a question of so that the overall picture could be

P. C. DOHERTY

Historical whodunnits and medieval crime fiction, in particular, have become hugely popular in recent years. This is very largely due to the success of Ellis Peters whose Cadfael novels have been bestsellers and have recently been translated to the television screen. Probably the best and most entertaining writer of medieval mysteries now at work is P.C. Doherty. This London headmaster has spent a lifetime studying the period and gained his Ph.D at Oxford in medieval history. His works are rooted in historical fact. Indeed several of his books interpret actual events - the mysterious death of Alexander III of Scotland, the murder of Edward II in Gloucestershire – with the eye and imagination of a seasoned crime writer. Doherty's best known medieval sleuth is Hugh Corbett, clerk of the English Chancery and master spy on behalf of the crown. Together with his bawdy, ex-felon sidekick Ranulf, Corbett must infiltrate treasonous gangs, avoid murderous satanists, sinister moneylenders and determined assassins to seek out the truth. Along the way Doherty provides vivid descriptions of the stench of fetid medieval gutters, the clinging chill of damp abbeys and the dark desolation of the ancient city of London after nightfall. In another series of books Doherty uses the characters from Chaucer's Canterbury Tales to narrate stories of murder and mystery during the evenings of their pilgrimage from Southwark to the shrine of St Thomas Becket. As in the Corbett novels the secret of his success lies in his firm grasp of the various aspects of medieval life and his ability to conjure up for the reader the sights, sounds and smells of a long-gone time.

An Ancient Evil
Headline pbk £4.99 0747243565

Angel of Death
Headline pbk £5.99 0747236941

The Assassin in the Greenwood
Headline pbk £5.99 0747242453

Crown in Darkness
Headline pbk £5.99 0747235058

The Devil's Hunt
Headline pbk £5.99 0747254397

Murder Wears A Cowl
Headline pbk £5.99 0747239916

The Prince of Darkness
Headline pbk £5.99 0747238669

The Rose Demon
Headline hbk £16.99 0747217661

Satan in St. Mary's
Headline pbk £5.99 0747234922

Satan's Fire
Headline pbk £5.99 0747249059

The Song of a Dark Angel
Headline pbk £5.99 0747244324

Spy in Chancery
Headline pbk £4.99 0747236151

A Tapestry of Murders
Headline pbk £5.99 0747245886

A Tournament of Murders
Headline pbk £4.99 0747249458

MURDER AND MAYHEM IN THE MIDDLE AGES

Nick Rennison speaks to P. C. Doherty about the attractions of historical crime fiction.

One of the big growth areas in crime fiction in recent years has been the historical mystery. Ellis Peters's Brother Cadfael has been joined by an entire cloisterful of clerical sleuths. Regency dandies and Ancient Roman reprobates alike have been unexpected successes as investigators. Even Jane Austen has made an appearance as a detective. Why is historical crime fiction so popular? No-one is better qualified to answer this question than P. C. Doherty who has been described as 'one of the best historical mystery writers around.' His medieval mysteries featuring Sir Hugh Corbett, King Edward I's Keeper of the Secret Seal, are justly popular and this prolific author has also written, under the pseudonyms of Paul Harding and Michael Clynes, another medieval series and a sequence about Sir Roger Shallot, intriguer and ne'er-do-well at Henry VIII's court. Somehow P. C. Doherty manages to fit his writing into the time he can spare from a demanding job as headmaster of a school in north-East London and I went to the school to discover his thoughts about historical crime fiction in general and medieval mysteries in particular.

My memories of visiting the headmaster's study in the past are not particularly happy ones. Nor do many of them include sitting in a comfortable armchair with a cup of coffee and a selection of chocolate biscuits while the headmaster talks to me about medieval England. This, however, is what happens on this occasion. On the walls are framed illustrations from the jackets of many of the Corbett books. On the bookshelves I can see copies of books from all three series – *The Assassin in the Greenwood*, *The House of the Red Slayer*, *The Grail Murders*. Paul Doherty leans over the large, solid desk in front of him and pins down the appeal of the historical mystery. 'There are two elements to it, I think. Firstly, everybody loves a puzzle, a whodunnit and a successful historical mystery has to work on that level. Secondly, a good historical mystery offers an experience of a different world to the one in which the reader lives, one which, in many ways, is alien to them. It introduces people to a new world. I think this is particularly true of the period I write about - the medieval era. The world of the future, science fiction, people have become accustomed to that, almost blasé about it, but the world of the past is different. Medieval England is more bizarre than science fiction and yet it's real.'

So what is it about the medieval world that interests people? 'Well, for one thing, there's the marvellous gothic atmosphere which attracts people. Cowled monks, forbidding castles, gloomy abbeys. Then there's the combination of extremes. It was a society of tremendous piety and faith and yet it was also a time of very dark and bloody deeds. The best illustration of this is Canterbury Cathedral. There's this beautiful building, raised to the greater glory of God, and it was there that one of the bloodiest murders of the times took place. The murder of Thomas à Becket.' And murder, of course, is the essential ingredient of crime fiction. 'Yes, and murder in medieval times lends itself to the classic style of detective story. You don't have police procedures, you don't have pathology. The detective has to solve the murder or the mystery by the application of logic and observation alone.'

Of course, the middle ages is a broad term. Paul Doherty's novels are set, more specifically, in the fourteenth century. I wondered why he'd picked the fourteenth century rather than any other. 'Because it's filled with characters that are ideal for fiction. This was Chaucer's society, after all. There are monks that have been killers, friars that are fornicators, bishops who are thoroughly corrupt.' Doherty did a doctorate at Oxford on Edward II's queen, Isabella, and realised at the time that the material cried out to be fictionalised. When you're writing an academic dissertation, you need to buttress everything you write with firm evidence. There's no room for speculation based on hints in the sources or conjectural reading between the lines. Yet Isabella's story - one of adultery, passion and likely murder - caught Doherty's imagination and was eventually the subject not only of his doctoral thesis but also of his first novel. The characters of the period obviously exist as real people for him. He talks vividly about Edward II's father, Edward I. 'He was a very hot-tempered man. He once threw his daughter's crown into the fire when she annoyed him. You can still read about it in the Household Accounts - Item : To the Mending of the Princess's Crown Thrown Into the Fire by her father, the King. You can just imagine the old clerk faithfully noting all the details down.' He laughs at the image he's conjured up. 'There was this tremendous rivalry between Edward and Philip the Fair of France and the letters between them are very revealing. There they are, politely writing to 'my dear brother in Christ' and you know that all the time they want to shake each other warmly by the throat.'

It's not just the great and the good of the fourteenth century who attract the novelist's eye. His research for the Corbett books and the Sorrowful Mysteries of Brother Athelstan leads him down some historical byways. 'There are all kinds of records - the letterbooks of London, as they're known, coroners' reports - which are filled with marvellous stories. There was one case where a man had a toilet at the top of his house and the toilet collapsed through the rest of the house. People were jerrybuilding you see. I put that directly into a novel. And the cases reported in the coroners' records, knife-fights in the city for instance, they're very specific. Ideal for a novelist. "Nick Rennison was drinking in the Silver Tabard tavern which stands at the corner of St. Paul's and Ludgate when Paul Doherty entered. Nick Rennison accused him of taking two ells of cloth from his store. He drew his dagger and slew the said Paul Doherty wherupon he fled to St. Mary-le-Bow church" and so on. Full of detail.'

Paul Doherty is planning a new series of historical mysteries, the first of which he has begun to write. In a change of direction this series is to be set in Ancient Egypt, another colourful society in which squalor and glory are mixed together. He will continue to write his medieval mysteries and continue to pursue his own fascination with the details of fourteenth century life. His enthusiasm for his subject is infectious. He is the kind of history teacher every pupil dreams of having but not every school possesses. He makes the past come to life. He has done so in our conversation and he does so in his novels. The best historical mysteries all do this and they combine that with the traditional pleasures, the intellectual puzzle, of the classic detective story of the golden age.

SIR ARTHUR CONAN DOYLE (1859–1930)

Doyle came from a family of artists and illustrators – his uncle worked for *Punch* from the time of its first publication and his grandfather was a celebrated political caricaturist in the era of Rowlandson and Cruickshank – but he trained originally as a doctor. He began writing in the eighteen eighties and Sherlock Holmes made his first appearance in *A Study in Scarlet* (1887). The character's huge popularity developed as short stories, later collected as *The Adventures of Sherlock Holmes* (1892) and *The Memoirs of Sherlock Holmes* (1894), appeared in the *Strand Magazine*. So great did Holmes's popularity grow that Doyle, who was a prolific writer in many other fields, became resentful that he was identified solely as the creator of the saturnine detective. He attempted to kill him off by sending him plunging over the Reichenbach Falls in the clutches of the criminal mastermind Professor Moriarty, but the public demanded his return and Doyle was obliged reluctantly to comply. Several further novels and collections of short stories appeared, including perhaps the most famous Holmes story *The Hound of the Baskervilles* (1902) in the years before Doyle's death in 1930. Sherlock Holmes, the supremely rational detective who is able to make the most startlingly accurate deductions from the flimsiest evidence, and Dr. Watson, the stolid, slightly obtuse narrator of the tales, are amongst the most famous and readily recognised fictional characters ever created. Their appeal to their original readers can be analysed historically. Lack of faith in the police and anxieties about the potential breakdown of law and order were commonplace at the time. It is surely no coincidence that the first Sherlock Holmes story appeared in the same year as the Bloody Sunday demonstration in Trafalgar Square, when police violently broke up a socialist demonstration against government policy in Ireland, and that the following year saw the police failure to capture Jack the Ripper. The idea of an omniscient detective, capable of solving even the most baffling of mysteries, must have provided reassurance to the middle class readers of *Strand Magazine*. Why the appeal has proved so long-lasting, why Holmes and Watson have appeared in so many different guises - in stage adaptations, films, televi-

The Adventures of Sherlock Holmes
Oxford UP pbk £3.99 0192823787
The Adventures of Sherlock Holmes
Penguin pbk £3.99 0140057242
The Casebook of Sherlock Holmes
Oxford UP pbk £3.99 0192823744
The Casebook of Sherlock Holmes
Penguin pbk £3.99 0140008055
The Complete Sherlock Holmes
Penguin pbk £9.99 0140056947
His Last Bow
Oxford UP pbk £3.99 0192823817
His Last Bow
Penguin pbk £3.99 0140057099
The Hound of the Baskervilles
Oxford UP pbk £3.99 0192823779
The Hound of the Baskervilles
Penguin pbk £3.99 0140001115
The Memoirs of Sherlock Holmes
Oxford UP pbk £3.99 0192823752

The Memoirs of Sherlock Holmes
Penguin pbk £3.99 0140007857

The Return of Sherlock Holmes
Oxford UP pbk £3.99 0192823760

The Return of Sherlock Holmes
Penguin pbk £3.99 0140057080

The Sign of Four
Oxford UP pbk £3.99 0192823795

The Sign of Four
Penguin pbk £3.99 0140058559

A Study in Scarlet
Oxford UP pbk £3.99 0192823809

A Study in Scarlet
Penguin pbk £3.99 0140057072

The Uncollected Sherlock Holmes
Penguin pbk £5.99 014006432X

The Valley of Fear
Oxford UP pbk £3.99 0192823825

The Valley of Fear
Penguin pbk £3.99 0140057102

sion series - and why there has been such a vast amount of Holmes-related material published over the years are more difficult questions to answer. The stories themselves often contain weak plots and repetitive dialogue but Holmes and Watson transcend them and have escaped the boundaries of the fiction in a way that few characters in English literature, except some of Shakespeare's and some of Dickens's, have done. It is safe to assume that they will remain semi-mythical figures for as long as detective fiction, of any kind, continues to be read.

'You will remember, Watson, how the dreadful business of the Abernetty family was first brought to my notice by the depth the parsley had sunk into the butter upon a hot summer day.'

Conan Doyle, *The Return of Sherlock Holmes*

SARAH DREHER

Sarah Dreher is a lesbian author who writes crime fiction with a lesbian heroine. This is true as far as it goes but is too limiting and constraining a description of a writer with a free-spirited and experimental approach to fiction. Her heroine Stoner McTavish is a strong-willed travel agent with a reluctantly accepted reputation as a solver of crimes. She has also been – such is the unconventional nature of Dreher's imagination – a time traveller, has discovered an alternative reality beneath Disney World and has received psychic messages from her Aunt Hermione. Dreher's first book and her 1996 book *Bad Company,* in which Stoner and her partner Gwen are asked to investigate the threats and small accidents that are plaguing a lesbian theatre company, show her skills as a crime writer. Her other books, especially *Gray Magic* and *Other Worlds*, challenge accepted categorisations by mixing the conventions of crime and gay fiction with those of contemporary fantasy writing. The result is a series of thoroughly amusing, intelligent and readable novels.

Bad Company
Women's Press pbk £6.99 0704344696

Captive in Time
New Victoria pbk £7.99 0934678227

Grey Magic
New Victoria pbk £7.99 0934678111

Otherworld
New Victoria pbk £8.99 0934678448

Stoner McTavish
Women's Press pbk £5.99 070434470X

STELLA DUFFY

In just three novels Stella Duffy has carved out a position for herself at the forefront of the new wave of British crime fiction and her dyke detective Saz Martin is an original and likeable heroine. Saz Martin's investigations into deceptions, betrayals and murders are not only cleverly constructed and psychologically compelling but conducted in recognisably nineties environs. Other crime writers have examined the worlds of psychotherapy, as Duffy does in *Wavewalker,* and the rock industry, as she does in *Beneath the Blonde,* but few have her ability to avoid embarrassing solecisms and to convey authenticity and conviction. Plus her books are witty, fast moving and filled with relishable dialogue and one-liners.

Beneath the Blonde
Serpent's Tail pbk £8.99
1852425423

Calendar Girl
Serpent's Tail pbk £7.99
1852423676

Wavewalker
Serpent's Tail pbk £8.99
1852425083

SARAH DUNANT

Hannah Wolfe has been described by one critic as 'one of the best private eyes, either sex, either side of the Atlantic'. She makes her first appearance in *Birthmarks*, in which her investigation of the disappearance of a young dancer leads her into some very murky and sinister waters indeed. Since then this cynical, wisecracking and laid-back heroine has appeared in several more novels in which Dunant has much fun subverting the clichés of the genre. The novels are, however, much more than tongue-in-cheek pastiche. As one would expect from Dunant, one-time presenter of BBC 2's *The Late Show*, the books are highly intelligent and combine barbed and funny observations about life, men and the deplorable state of the world with genuinely pacy action and mystery.

Birth Marks
Penguin pbk £5.99 0140147667
Fatlands
Penguin pbk £5.99 0140230491
Under My Skin
Penguin pbk £5.99 0140247394

RUTH DUDLEY EDWARDS

Ruth Dudley Edwards has written a number of well-received biographies and is the author of the official history of that most serious of magazines *The Economist*. In her crime fiction she is far from serious. Her series of books featuring Robert Amiss, ex-civil servant and unofficial troubleshooter to the formidable Baroness Ida 'Jack' Troutbeck, turn a farcical and satirical eye on all those institutions which remain bastions of the British establishment – the Foreign Office, Cambridge colleges, the church and gentlemen's clubs. These ingenious burlesques succeed both as well-plotted mysteries and as laugh-aloud comic fiction.

Matricide at St. Martha's
HarperCollins pbk £4.99
0006493289
Publish and Be Murdered
HarperCollins hbk £15.99
0002325985
Ten Lords A-Leaping
HarperCollins pbk £4.99
0006498051

JAMES ELLROY

After a series of exemplary tough guy novels, including the Lloyd Hopkins cop thrillers, James Ellroy finally achieved his full potential with the peerless *The Black Dahlia*. Based on a real-life unsolved murder in Los Angeles just after World War II, the book quickly spins into a relentless, dark revision of history. Real people – Howard Hughes, movie stars, mobsters – interact with Ellroy's bleak and obsessed fictional creations. A further three volumes, each more feverish than the last, consolidated Ellroy's reputation as a foul-mouthed latterday Balzac, moving dozens of characters through unbelievably involved plots over a period of decades. *American Tabloid*, a sequel to the LA Quartet takes the story into the political arena. Ellroy's characters, J. Edgar Hoover, the mafia, the Cubans and the Kennedys all converge cataclysmically. The last chapter of the book is set fatefully in Dallas on the 22nd November 1963. Ellroy is candid about his preoccupation with the Black Dahlia case. His own mother was murdered when he was a child and, as in the Black Dahlia case, the murderer was never apprehended. His most recent book *My Dark Places* is autobiography rather than fiction and deals unflinchingly with his depraved criminal youth, his rehabilitation and his recent attempts to solve his mother's murder. It is a hellish account of a troubled life but it is essential reading.

American Tabloid
Arrow pbk £5.99 0099893207

The Big Nowhere
Arrow pbk £6.99 0099366614

The Black Dahlia
Arrow pbk £5.99 0099366517

Brown's Requiem
Arrow pbk £5.99 0099649012

Clandestine
Arrow pbk £5.99 0099226227

Dick Contino's Blues
Arrow pbk £5.99 0099410117

LA Confidential
Arrow pbk £6.99 0099366711

LA Noir
Arrow pbk £9.99 009925590X

My Dark Places
Arrow pbk £6.99 0099549611

White Jazz
Arrow pbk £6.99 0099649403

LOREN ESTLEMAN

Estleman once described the Motor City as 'the place where the American Dream stalled and sat rusting in the rain' and his dyspeptic view of Detroit has stood him in very good stead. Only Raymond Chandler's love/hate relationship with Los Angeles has mined as rich a vein as Estleman's. The Chandler comparison extends beyond eloquently expressed urban disaffection, however, as Estleman has a worthy substitute for Philip Marlowe in Amos Walker. Walker is a private eye in the classic mould – tough, stubborn, handy with a wisecrack and, when the pace hots up, armed with either a gun or (in dire emergencies) a slug or two from the office bottle. Cynical yet ruefully honest, Walker avoids Marlowe's (or Chandler's) tendency to feel sorry for himself. Throughout the ten Walker novels and the many other noirish books Estleman has written, whether they are set in the Prohibition twenties (*Whiskey River*), the fifties boom years (*Edsel*) or the political unrest and violence of the sixties (*Downriver*), there is one constant: the Motor City itself.

City of Widows
Pan pbk £4.99 0330343424
Whiskey River
Little Brown hbk £12.99 0356200396

*American editions of other Estleman
titles may be available in larger
Waterstones branches*

'It was a garage apartment, shack sized, at the rear of a big Victorian house. Lights were burning inside; Lee, yawning, said, 'Good guy – bad guy', and rang the buzz.' James Ellroy, *The Black Dahlia*

JANET EVANOVICH

Stephanie Plum is one of the more engaging and vivid female characters in contemporary American crime fiction. The tyro bounty hunter, who works for her cousin's bail-bondsman operation, tracking down a collection of misfits ranging through the deeply sad to the very bad, has appeared so far in three books by Janet Evanovich. Big of hair, high of blood sugar level and possessed of a stroppy, smart-mouthed, New Jersey humour Plum is an inspired creation. Not only does she have to deal with absconding criminals but, far more demandingly, her mother, her Grandma Mazur, whose hobby is reading obituaries and meeting her contemporaries at funeral homes to inspect the corpse and critique the arrangements, and Joe Morelli, the cop with the best ass in New Jersey. Evanovich has skilfully and wittily created an ensemble piece in each of the novels so far, in which felons, family and other characters spar and interact.

One for the Money
Penguin pbk £5.99 0140252924

Two for the Dough
Penguin pbk £5.99 0140255559

Three to Get Deadly
Penguin pbk £5.99 0140256083

'Okay, who was I trying to kid? I was contemplating stealing Morelli's car. Not steal, I reasoned. Commandeer. After all I was a bounty hunter, and probably I could commandeer a car if an emergency arose. I glanced over at the Nova. Looked like an emergency to me.'

Janet Evanovich, *One for the Money*

ELIZABETH EYRE

Under the pseudonym of Elizabeth Eyre, Jill Staynes and Margaret Storey, authors of the witty and engaging series about the modern detective, Superintendent Bone, have turned their attention to historical crime fiction. Set in an imaginatively realised Italian Renaissance, the series is notable for its adroit plotting and for the strength of its central character, the enigmatic Sigismondo, a former mercenary as unfathomable as some of the mysteries he investigates.

Axe for an Abbot
Headline pbk £5.99 0747251630

Bravo for the Bride
Headline pbk £4.99 0747245894

Curtains for the Cardinal
Headline pbk £4.99 0747241090

Death of a Duchess
Headline pbk £4.99 0747237484

Dirge for a Doge
Headline pbk £5.99 0747255008

Poison for the Prince
Headline pbk £4.99 0747242143

ROBERT FERRIGNO

One of the most dazzling crime writers to emerge from America in many years, Ferrigno has captured the sultry allure of Southern California and squeezed every last ounce of noir from it. All four of his novels are set in and around Los Angeles and are full of the grotesqueries that seem to characterise that city. *Horse Latitudes* features drug dealers, steroid-popping body builders with much more brawn than brain, a big game-hunting pharmacologist who's also trying to crack the secret of eternal youth, cops both good and bad, and the book's 'hero' Danny, a former dope-dealer whose ex-wife has disappeared, leaving behind a blood-spattered corpse in her luxury house. *The Cheshire Moon* and *Dead Man's Dance* introduce the reader to Quinn, a charming and likeable journalist whose glory days are long behind him. In disgrace, Quinn is reduced to interviewing minor celebrities and trying to sort out his tangled love life. Sharing the pages with Quinn are a psychotic ex-footballer who is now security guard for a talk-show hostess, the State Governor who also happens to be the husband of the talk-show hostess, a beautiful photographer and a pair of sociopathic killers. As they all parade through the books, cruising the streets and beaches of La-La Land, a picture emerges of paradise somehow transplanted to hell. In his most recent book, *Dead Silent*, Ferrigno turns his gaze on the LA music scene as Nick Carbonne, record producer and one-hit wonder, tries to discover why his wife is in the hot-tub with his old friend Perry and why they're both naked and very dead. Ferrigno digs brilliantly beneath the showbiz mythologising, the sun and the surfing wonderland of California to reveal the darknesses beneath.

The Cheshire Moon
Simon & Schuster pbk £4.99 0671850849

Dead Man's Dance
Simon & Schuster pbk £5.99 0671854836

Robert Ferrigno's most recent novel, Dead Silent, *is currently unavailable in the UK but some Waterstone's branches may stock the American edition.*

ELIZABETH FERRARS

Author of more than sixty novels and a founding member of the Crime Writers' Association, Elizabeth Ferrars has been a successful practitioner of the traditional mystery story. Her style of writing and her use of the long-established formulas of the genre are, perhaps, slightly unfashionable but her competent plotting and believable characters make her a rewarding read for admirers of the 'comfortable' crime story.

Alibi for a Witch
Hodder pbk £4.99 0340574089

The Cup and the Lip
Hodder pbk £4.99 0340596511

Don't Monkey With Murder
Hodder pbk £4.99 0340607513

Foot in the Grave
Hodder pbk £4.99 0340515902

The Lying Voices
Hodder pbk £5.99 0340640553

The Milk of Human Kindness
Hodder pbk £4.99 0340637986

Murder Among Friends
Hodder pbk £4.99 0340430532

Murder of a Suicide
Hodder pbk £4.99 0340624531

Neck in a Noose
Hodder pbk £5.99 0340607505

A Tale of Two Murders
Hodder pbk £4.99 0340582588

DICK FRANCIS

The world of horses and horse racing is one that Dick Francis knows from the inside which gives his books an authenticity that is hard to match. Francis, who was champion jockey in 1953/4, was forced to retire from racing after a serious fall and this was the impetus to begin a second career as a writer. Journalism led to his first novel, *Dead Cert* which appeared in 1963, and a new novel has famously appeared at a rate of one a year ever since. They are more suspense thrillers than classic whodunits, and the male first person narrator often has to battle through considerable physical hardship before winning through in the end. The similarities in protagonists and milieu (jockeys, trainers, owners and racetracks), mean that readers always know what they are getting with Francis, but his sharp dialogue and fast plotting never flag and raise him above his imitators.

Banker
Pan pbk £4.99 0330281992

Blood Sport
Pan pbk £5.99 0330023462

Bolt
Pan pbk £4.99 0330301381

Bonecrack
Pan pbk £5.99 0330234471

Break In
Pan pbk £4.99 033029380X

Come to Grief
Pan pbk £5.99 0330347772

Comeback
Pan pbk £4.99 0330324861

The Danger
Pan pbk £5.99 033028505X

Dead Cert
Pan pbk £5.99 0330246216

Decider
Pan pbk £4.99 0330335685

Driving Force
Pan pbk £5.99 0330329510

The Edge
Pan pbk £4.99 0330310712

Enquiry
Pan pbk £5.99 0330026747

Flying Finish
Pan pbk £5.99 0330021117

For Kicks
Pan pbk £5.99 0330105965

Forfeit
Pan pbk £5.99 0330025325

High Stakes
Pan pbk £4.99 0330248367

Hot Money
Pan pbk £4.99 0330305050

In the Frame
Pan pbk £5.99 0330253077

Knockdown
Pan pbk £4.99 0330246208

Longshot
Pan pbk £4.99 0330319582

Nerve
Pan pbk £5.99 0330246224

Odds Against
Pan pbk £5.99 0330105973

Proof
Pan pbk £5.99 033029069X

Rat Race
Pan pbk £4.99 0330029665

Reflex
Pan pbk £4.99 0330266624

Risk
Pan pbk £4.99 0330257129

Slay Ride
Pan pbk £4.99 0330242199

Smokescreen
Pan pbk £5.99 0330239171

Straight
Pan pbk £5.99 0330314424

To the Hilt
M. Joseph pbk £8.99 0718142438

Trial Run
Pan pbk £4.99 0330259830

Twice Shy
Pan pbk £5.99 0330269186

Whip Hand
Pan pbk £4.99 0330263064

Wild Horses
Pan pbk £5.99 0330341421

JOHN FRANCOME

John Francome used to be a National Hunt jockey and he has followed in the footsteps of Dick Francis in carving out a second career as a writer of exciting and tautly written mysteries and thrillers set in the world of racing. Since the mid-eighties he has published a series of such novels, at first in conjunction with other writers, but latterly under his own name alone.

Blood Stock
Headline pbk £5.99 0747234167

Break Neck
Headline pbk £5.99 0747247048

Dead Ringer
Headline pbk £5.99 0747249415

Declared Dead
Headline pbk £5.99 0747232512

Eavesdropper
Headline pbk £5.99 0747241260

Outsider
Headline pbk £6.99 0747243751

Riding High
Headline pbk £5.99 0747241279

Rough Ride
Headline pbk £5.99 0747240868

Stone Cold
Headline pbk £5.99 0747234833

Stud Poker
Headline pbk £5.99 0747237549

ANTONIA FRASER

The respected historian, who has written biographies of Cromwell and Mary Queen of Scots and whose most recent work was a study of the Gunpowder Plot, has also written a sequence of light but enjoyable detective novels. Her glamorous heroine, sleuth and television reporter Jemima Shore, moves among the higher echelons of the media, academic and social worlds, encountering murder and mystery with alarming regularity.

The Cavalier Case
Mandarin pbk £4.99 0749303247

Quiet as a Nun
Mandarin pbk £4.99 0749308559

Cool Repentance
Mandarin pbk £4.99 0749308532

A Splash of Red
Mandarin pbk £5.99 0749308508

Oxford Blood
Mandarin pbk £4.99 0749308516

The Wild Island
Mandarin pbk £5.99 0749308524

Political Death
Mandarin pbk £4.99 0749319143

NICHOLAS FREELING

Nicholas Freeling used to be best known for the stories featuring the Dutch police inspector Van der Valk and several TV series, based on them and starring Barry Foster, were made. The Van der Valk books are now out of print but Freeling has created other characters, including the French detective Henri Carstang, and some of these titles are still available. Like those of Simenon, many of Freeling's stories are based on the patient investigation of an often sordid crime and are firmly in the tradition of the *roman policier.*

A Dwarf Kingdom
Warner pbk £5.99 0751518670

The Pretty How Town
Warner pbk £4.99 0751501611

The Seacoast of Bohemia
Warner pbk £5.99 0751514942

You Who Know
Warner pbk £4.99 0751510289

'Downtown Judy and I hadn't been in bed long when the phone rang. It cut through the two of us like a shrimping knife.'

**Kinky Freidman,
A Case of Lone Star**

KINKY FRIEDMAN

Kinky Friedman first made a name as an unusual country rock singer in Austin, Texas where he fronted a band called *The Texas Jewboys* and recorded such classics as 'They Don't Make Jews Like Jesus Anymore.' When he turned his attention to crime-writing it was a certainty that his work in the genre would be equally unusual. The protagonist of his novels is based on Kinky himself, bears the same name, has the same former occupation and a line in wisecracks worthy of the classic hardboiled private dicks. His inventive and ornate humour is often directed at the sinful pleasures and penitential pains of drinking, smoking, sex and substance abuse. The novels are set in New York and somewhere amidst the tequila and the cigars and the gags there is usually a body or two since, in the novels at least, the Kinkster is now more of a detective than a singer. Despite his emphasis on the episodic and the goonish, Friedman does have a firm grasp on his plots and the cracking wise never entirely overwhelms the effective and satisfying mysteries that he constructs. However Kinky remains most refreshing as an alternative to the more grim and dour writers of American crime and memorable for the chutzpah with which he has remade the detective hero in his own image.

Armadillos and Old Lace
Faber pbk £5.99 0571174620
Elvis, Jesus and Coca-Cola
Faber pbk £5.99 0571171923
God Bless John Wayne
Faber pbk £5.99 0571179479
Greenwich Killing Time
Faber pbk £5.99 0571191347
Kinky Friedman Crime Club
Faber pbk £9.99 0571168000
Love Song of J. Edgar Hoover
Faber pbk £8.99 0571178669
More Kinky Friedman
Faber pbk £8.99 0571170307
Roadkill
Faber pbk £8.99 0571192203

FRANCES FYFIELD

Frances Fyfield has long had a reputation as one of the most subtle and intelligent crime writers in Britain, capable of creating a dark and stylish, psychological suspense. Many of her novels feature the team of Crown Prosecutor Helen West and senior policeman Geoffrey Bailey. Together they shed light on the crimes central to the narratives but the emphasis in Fyfield's multi-layered and richly characterised novels is as much on understanding and revealing ordinary and extraordinary human behaviour as it is on the conventional solution to a mystery. This rewarding writer deserves a wide audience. She has also written novels under the name of Frances Hegarty.

A Clear Conscience
Transworld pbk £4.99 0552142956
Deep Sleep
Mandarin pbk £5.99 0749308915
Perfectly Pure and Good
Transworld pbk £5.99 0552141747
A Question of Guilt
Mandarin pbk £5.99 0749310200
Shadow Play
Transworld pbk £4.99 0552140430
Shadows on the Mirror
Mandarin pbk £5.99 0749310219
Without Consent
Transworld pbk £5.99 0552145122

ERLE STANLEY GARDNER

(1889–1970)
After Sherlock Holmes the second most popular character in crime fiction, judged by total sales over the years, is Erle Stanley Gardner's master of courtroom drama Perry Mason. Gardner began writing for the pulps in the twenties and thirties but his career took off when he used his legal experience and his growing skill in devising tortuous plots to create the Perry Mason novels. Eventually there were more than eighty titles in the sequence and the lawyer was played by Raymond Burr in a long-running TV series. Despite their status as past bestsellers, the Perry Mason novels are no longer in print in this country but it seems unlikely that there will not be some future revival of interest and that Mason will not get the opportunity to spring his courtroom surprises on another generation of readers.

American editions of the Perry Mason novels may be available on import from some Waterstone's shops.

JONATHAN GASH

Lovejoy is best remembered from the TV series of the late eighties and early nineties in which Ian McShane played the shady and lecherous antiques dealer whose dodgy business ethics led him into any number of tight corners. The character originated in novels by Jonathan Gash and a few of these enjoyably high camp tales of low life are still in print. Gash has also written other thrillers and mysteries.

Different Women Dancing
Macmillan hbk £15.99 0333710371

Gold from Gemini
Arrow pbk £4.99 0099463504

The Grace in Older Women
Arrow pbk £4.99 0099526913

Moonspender
Arrow pbk £4.99 0099523701

The Possessions of a Lady
Arrow pbk £5.99 0099791714

The Very Last Gambado
Arrow pbk £4.99 0099740206

ELIZABETH GEORGE

Elizabeth George was working as a creative writing teacher in California when she burst on the crime writing stage with her spectacular debut novel *A Great Deliverance*, the first of what has become a series of police procedurals set in contemporary England. It won a number of awards for best first crime novel in both Europe and the US and subsequent titles have also proved to be prizewinners. The protagonists of all her books are the elegant Detective Inspector Thomas Lynley, who also happens to be the 8th Earl of Asherton, and his partner, the working-class Detective Sergeant Barbara Havers. Thrown together accidentally in their first case, they view one another with suspicion (indeed outright dislike on Havers's part) but the suspicion develops into a sustaining friendship in the course of their many investigations. The books also contain a number of other recurring characters who move in and out of the plots of many of the novels, giving substance to the sense of complex personal relationships and histories which helps make George's work so compelling. Her novels are satisfying works of crime fiction which also examine serious themes of friendship and loyalty, love and betrayal, the debt owed to parents by children (and vice versa), unsentimentiously and unpompously.

Deception on his Mind
Hodder pbk £9.99 0340689307

For the Sake of Elena
Bantam pbk £5.99 0553402374

A Great Deliverance
Bantam pbk £5.99 0553175106

In the Presence of the Enemy
Bantam pbk £5.99 0553408461

Missing Joseph
Bantam pbk £5.99 0553402382

Payment in Blood
Bantam pbk £5.99 0553175114

Playing for the Ashes
Bantam pbk £5.99 0553408453

A Suitable Vengeance
Bantam pbk £5.99 0553401688

Well-Schooled in Murder
Bantam pbk £5.99 055340167X

MICHAEL GILBERT

Gilbert was a lawyer who published detective fiction over a number of decades and in a variety of sub-genres. All his books, whether they are the police procedurals featuring Inspector Petrella, the novels involving the counter-intelligence agents Calder and Behrens or the other works that this versatile writer produced, are densely plotted and peopled by convincing and well-rounded characters.

The novels of Michael Gilbert are not available in paperback in this country. Some larger branches of Waterstone's may stock American editions of his work.

DAVID GOODIS (1917–1967)

One of the great romantics of hard-boiled fiction, Goodis remains little known in the UK. Best remembered for Down There (filmed by Truffaut as Shoot the Piano Player) Goodis first tasted cinematic success in the forties when classic film noir duo Bogart and Bacall starred in the movie version of his book Dark Passage. Goodis moved to Hollywood to be a screenwriter but the shallowness of Tinseltown grated and he quit in 1950 to return to crime writing. The typical Goodis protagonist is someone who has fallen from grace, a once successful man brought low, someone who drifts through nowhere jobs and lonely city streets in a state of quiet despair and guilt about his past life. Usually Goodis allows the alcoholics, musicians and rooming-house relics who people his stories one moment of redemptive triumph over the corruption and violence that surround them before they meet their end. His work is lushly sentimental yet it is tempered by his genuine skill in depicting some of the grimy reality of life in the great American cities and by his ability to embody in his novels, from Street of No Return to Nightfall, a particular, romantic urban sensibility.

The work of David Goodis is currently unavailable in the UK. Imports of American editions of his books may be available in some larger Waterstone's branches.

PAULA GOSLING

Born in Detroit, Paula Gosling moved to this country in 1964 and has worked as a full-time writer since 1979. She has won both the John Creasey Award for the Best First Crime Novel and the CWA Gold Dagger. Her earlier novels were very fast-paced suspense novels which moved into the territory occupied by the out-and-out thriller. These are currently unavailable. Her most recent books are set in the Great Lakes community of Blackwater Bay and a critic wrote that they read 'as if Garrison Keillor was meeting Miss Marple for the first time.' They have more edge and bite than this suggests but do have a particular charm of their own.

The Dead of Winter
Warner pbk £5.99 0751516783
Fair Game
Warner pbk £5.99 0751517070

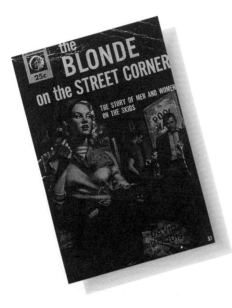

LAWRENCE GOUGH

Gough is an award-winning Canadian author of ten crime novels featuring police detectives Claire Parker and Jack Willows. Set in Vancouver, the books have plenty of humour and charm, much of the latter due to the fact that Parker and Willows, as well as being partners, are also lovers. An instantly likeable double act, the pair are a kind of Nick and Nora Charles (from Hammett's *The Thin Man*) of the nineties, together with a uniquely Canadian slant. With a solid hard-boiled edge to them, the novels are skilfully plotted and full of the required twists and turns. They're also topped off with generous helpings of Gough's biting wit and convincing scenes of action and violence.

Accidental Deaths
Gollancz pbk £4.99 0575056134

Serious Crimes
Gollancz pbk £4.99 0575054441

SUE GRAFTON

The first book in Sue Grafton's alphabet series, *A for Alibi*, was published in 1986 and met with immediate critical success. However some of the same critics who praised the novel also cast doubts on Grafton's staying power, suggesting that the former scriptwriter would be unable to keep up such a high standard for another twenty five books. More than ten years later and half the alphabet finished, Grafton has shown that she is a top-class crime writer whose books increase in vigour and freshness as the series continues. Set in California the novels all feature private eye Kinsey Millhone and it is the realism of her character that gives the series much of its originality. Millhone is a logical, patient and methodical investigator who tackles her cases of fraud, adultery and missing persons with a determination to uncover the truth whatever it may be. She is confident and assured. As the cases become more sinister, and increasingly involve murder, Millhone's character changes too. She experiences fear and anxiety and her own instincts and emotions clash with her desire to solve the case. Grafton skilfully balances plot and character and, as the story becomes more involved, the reader becomes absorbed not only in the solution to the case Millhone is investigating but also in how Millhone herself will deal with the twists and turns of the case. In developing her books into one of the finest series of private eye novels available at present, Grafton has shown that the alphabet can be readily completed.

A is For Alibi
Pan pbk £4.99 033031582X

B is For Burglar
Pan pbk £4.99 0330315838

C is For Corpse
Pan pbk £4.99 0330315846

D is For Deadbeat
Pan pbk £4.99 0330315854

E is For Evidence
Pan pbk £4.99 0330315862

F is For Fugitive
Pan pbk £4.99 0330315870

G is For Gumshoe
Pan pbk £4.99 0330317237

H is For Homicide
Pan pbk £4.99 0330321951

I is For Innocent
Pan pbk £4.99 0330326430

J is For Judgement
Pan pbk £4.99 0330333402

K is For Killer
Pan pbk £4.99 0330334808

L is For Lawless
Pan pbk £5.99 0330334816

M is For Malice
Pan pbk £5.99 0330348760

CAROLINE GRAHAM

Although not an instantly familiar name, even to some crime buffs, Caroline Graham has been described by one critic as 'the best detective writer since Agatha Christie' and her first novel *The Killings at Badger's Drift* was selected by the CWA as one of the best one hundred crime novels of all time. This book, like most of her others, is set in a small, apparently close-knit community, which a crime and its investigation reveals to be riven with petty jealousies and rivalries. Five out of her seven books feature the watchful and sympathetic Chief Inspector Barnaby and the pragmatic Sergeant Troy of Causton CID whose investigations uncover the tensions beneath apparently tranquil surfaces. Crimes are shown to be the result of ordinary human hopes, fears and failings rather than grand passions and the apparently trivial is seen to be the trigger for murder. Caroline Graham's books combine first-rate characterisation and plotting with wit and a capacity for keeping the reader guessing to the last page. She is a writer who demonstrates that the tradition of classic English detective fiction is still alive and well.

Death in Disguise
Headline pbk £5.99 0747239746

Death of a Hollow Man
Headline pbk £5.99 0747233500

The Envy of the Stranger
Headline pbk £5.99 0747243972

Faithful Unto Death
Headline pbk £5.99 0747249709

The Killings at Badger's Drift
Headline pbk £5.99 0747232334

Murder at Madingley Grange
Headline pbk £5.99 0747235961

Written in Blood
Headline pbk £5.99 0747246645

ANN GRANGER

One of the best examples of a crime writer who has taken the classic English village detective story and brought it up to date, Ann Granger has written a number of novels featuring Superintendent Alan Markby and his girlfriend, civil servant Meredith Mitchell. These books, with their understated humour, deft plotting and endearingly eccentric characterisation, are amongst the most engaging of those modern crime stories written in the tradition of the golden age of English detective fiction. Ann Granger has also just published *Asking for Trouble*, the first in a new series featuring a young private investigator Fran Varady.

Asking for Trouble
Headline hbk £16.99 0747218676

Candle for a Corpse
Headline pbk £5.99 0747249083

Cold in the Earth
Headline pbk £5.99 074723874X

A Fine Place for Death
Headline pbk £5.99 0747244626

Flowers for his Funeral
Headline pbk £5.99 0747247706

Murder Among Us
Headline pbk £5.99 0747240434

Say It With Poison
Headline pbk £5.99 0747237069

A Season for Murder
Headline pbk £5.99 0747237158

A Touch of Mortality
Headline pbk £5.99 074725186X

Where Old Bones Lie
Headline pbk £5.99 0747242976

A Word After Dying
Headline pbk £5.99 0747251878

D. M. GREENWOOD

D. M. Greenwood has worked for a number of years as an ecclesiastical civil servant in the Diocese of Rochester. Her lively and entertaining novels featuring the formidable Deacon Theodora Braithwaite, of the inner-city parish of St Sylvester's, have revived the traditions of the clerical mystery.

Clerical Errors
Headline pbk £4.99 0747235821

Every Deadly Sin
Headline pbk £4.99 0747249849

Heavenly Vices
Headline hbk £16.99 0747217580

Holy Terrors
Headline pbk £4.99 0747244960

Idol Bones
Headline pbk £5.99 0747240582

Mortal Spoils
Headline pbk £4.99 0747251908

Unholy Ghosts
Headline pbk £4.99 074723583X

MARTHA GRIMES

Martha Grimes's series of titles featuring Scotland Yard Chief Superintendent Richard Jury, each of which refers to a genuine but unusually named pub in this country, combines quirky humour and characterisation with thorough research and clever plotting.

The Anodyne Necklace
Headline pbk £4.99 0747234019

The Deer Leap
Headline pbk £4.99 0747230323

The Dirty Duck
Headline pbk £4.99 0747230048

The End of the Pier
Headline pbk £5.99 0747242372

The Five Bells and Bladebone
Headline pbk £5.99 0747231699

Help the Poor Struggler
Headline pbk £4.99 0747230374

The Horse You Came In On
Headline pbk £5.99 0747242216

Hotel Paradise
Headline pbk £5.99 0747251355

I Am the Only Running Footman
Headline pbk £4.50 0747231036

Jerusalem Inn
Headline pbk £4.99 0747230366

The Man With a Load of Mischief
Headline pbk £5.99 0747230358

The Old Contemptibles
Headline pbk £6.99 0747236984

The Old Fox Deceiv'd
Headline pbk £5.99 0747230331

The Old Silent
Headline pbk £5.99 0747234450

Rainbow's End
Headline pbk £5.99 0747251347

65

ROBERT VAN GULIK

Robert Van Gulik had the superb idea of recasting a number of classical Chinese folk stories into the form of detective fiction, seen through the eyes of Judge Dee. Original stories followed and the books achieved a worldwide success, largely because of van Gulik's strong characterisation of Dee and the insights his carefully researched stories offered into the customs and culture of ancient China.

Celebrated Cases of Judge Dee
Dover pbk £6.95 0486233375

The Chinese Bell Murders
University of Chicago P pbk £7.25
0226848620

The Chinese Gold Murders
University of Chicago P pbk £5.50
0226848647

The Chinese Lake Murders
University of Chicago P pbk £6.25
0226848655

The Chinese Maze Murders
University of Chicago P pbk £7.95
0226848787

The Chinese Nail Murders
University of Chicago P pbk £7.25
0226848639

The Haunted Monastery
Warner pbk £4.99 0751509620

The Lacquer Screen
Warner pbk £4.99 0751509612

Murder in Canton
University of Chicago P pbk £5.50
0226848744

Poets and Murder
University of Chicago P pbk £6.25
0226848760

The Willow Pattern
University of Chicago P pbk £4.75
0226848752

JAMES HALL

There are obvious comparisons to be made between the work of James Hall and that of Carl Hiaasen. Both authors write laugh-aloud funny books about over-the-top crime in Florida but the differences are also marked. Hiaasen's background is journalistic and his concerns are largely metropolitan. Hall is a poet by profession and his eco-conscience is stirred by the damage being inflicted on the natural habitats of the state. Hall's principal character is Thorn, an almost feral, sun-bleached loner who lives in the wilds of Florida. In Hall's first novel, *Under Cover of Daylight,* Thorn, who has severed his link with society by murdering the man who killed his parents in a drink-driving incident, is further alienated by the murder of his drug-smuggling foster mother. Vividly coloured mayhem ensues as does some kind of redemption. Thorn and his sometime sidekick, the neurotic cop Sugarman, are central in most of Hall's work and lurk in the background even of those novels which are not part of the series. Even if Hall's prose was not as gorgeous as it is, the Thorn novels would be required reading for their skewed characterisation. The villains are frequently likeable - intelligently and entertainingly wicked rather than simply thuggish. And the good guys are endearingly ramshackle too. *Gone Wild* may be the only crime novel ever written in which one of the most sympathetic heroes is an orang-outan.

Bones of Coral
Mandarin pbk £4.99 074930636X

Buzz Cut
Mandarin pbk £5.99 0749323728

Gone Wild
Mandarin pbk £5.99 0749321121

Hard Aground
Mandarin pbk £4.99 0749313250

Squall Line
Mandarin pbk £4.99 0749302496

Under Cover of Daylight
Mandarin pbk £4.99 0749308621

DASHIELL HAMMETT (1894-1961)

Dashiell Hammett would probably not have liked Cluedo. The murders in his stories were not committed by Colonel Mustard, in the library, with the candlestick. Raymond Chandler acknowledged Hammett's influence on his own work and wrote, 'Hammett took murder out of the Venetian vase and dropped it into the alley . . . (he) gave murder back to the people who commit it for reasons, not just to provide a corpse; and with the means at hand.'

In the course of about fifty short stories written between 1923 and 1929 and five novels produced in the years between 1929 and 1934, Hammett defined the hard-boiled private eye genre. Writing in the golden age of the pulp magazines, he frequently produced a story a month for *Black Mask*. Since the pulps paid no more than $200 a story, only a prolific writer could make a living. No doubt the need to sell each story to the editor and grab the attention of the reading public contributed to Hammett's efficient and action-packed style.

Most of the stories feature 'The Continental Op' who 'is a little man going forward day after day through mud and blood and death and deceit - as callous and brutal and cynical as necessary - towards a dim goal, with nothing to push or pull him towards it except he's been paid to reach it.' Less moral and thoughtful than Philip Marlowe, not even allowed a name (he works for the Continental Detective Agency) the Op is not much better than the criminals he faces, perhaps only different because he works for wages. He is the precursor of amoral enforcers from Mickey Spillane's Mike Hammer to Robocop. Hammett slowly elaborated his style to allow the Op and his other main characters, Sam Spade (*The Maltese Falcon*) and Nick Charles (*The Thin Man*) to develop feelings, a luxury in a tough-guy short story but necessary in a novel. Spade and Charles are more rounded characters with an existence outside the plot.

A new language grew with this new type of story, a dense stripped-down American that didn't interrupt the headlong rush of the plot. 'He put these people down on paper as they are, and he made them talk and think in the language they customarily used for these purposes.' (Chandler again) 'Another car came round the limousine and charged us. Out of it, gunfire.' (Red Harvest) This is writing for people who must think quickly and act quicker.

Hammett lived from 1894 to 1961 but wrote crime fiction for only twelve years. He was born in rural Maryland and after leaving school worked in a variety of jobs before he joined the Pinkerton's National Detective Service in 1915. An experienced agent, James Wright, taught him the tricks of the trade, and later provided a model for the Op. After a short period of war service he returned to Pinkerton's but contracted TB and had to resign. In 1922 he started writing advertising copy and stories. After *The Thin Man* appeared in 1934 he spent most of the rest of the thirties screenwriting in Hollywood, but by 1941 Hammett had effectively stopped writing.

In 1930 Hammett started a relationship with the writer Lillian Hellman that would last the rest of his life and, during the 1930s, he became an active supporter of the Communist Party. Despite recurring TB he rejoined the army from 1942 to 1945. Hammett smoked and drank heavily, suffered serious ill-health and could not find work because of his political beliefs. He was jailed for five months in 1951 for refusing to co-operate with the House Un-American Activities Committee. He died a recluse, heavily in debt, a sad end for a great writer of distinctively American fiction.

The Big Knockover and Other Stories
Penguin pbk £6.99 0140029419

The Four Great Novels
Picador pbk £10.99 0330268503

The Thin Man
Penguin pbk £5.99 0140000143

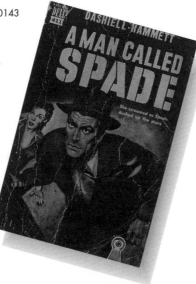

JOSEPH HANSEN

Dave Brandstetter is the humane and likeable hero of Hansen's novels, an insurance claims investigator whose job means he pounds those (still) mean streets of Los Angeles. He is also, though ruggedly masculine and not averse to the fisticuffs and dustups that occasionally accompany the territory, thoroughly and contentedly gay. In 1970, when the first Brandstetter novel was published, this was not common in a private eye of any kind. In the years since, more and more detectives, especially female ones, have come out of the closet but few of the newer writers with gay protagonists can match Hansen for the excellence of his prose and for the skill with which he has reworked the classic American private-eye novel.

A Country of Old Men
No Exit Press pbk £4.99
1874061068

Death Claims
No Exit Press pbk £4.99
1874061629

Fadeout
No Exit Press pbk £4.99
1874061610

The Man Everyone Was Afraid Of
No Exit Press pbk £4.99
1874061661

Skinflick
No Exit Press pbk £4.99
187406167X

Troublemaker
No Exit Press pbk £4.99
1874061653

PAUL HARDING

Paul Harding is the pseudonym under which the prolific P. C. Doherty has produced his series *The Sorrowful Mysteries of Brother Athelstan*. These historical crime novels, set in the late fourteenth century, feature the large, jovial but shrewd Coroner of the City of London, Sir John Cranston and his secretarius, Brother Athelstan of St Erconwald's. As in his other work the author displays his deep knowledge of the period and the pomp and poverty of the middle ages are vividly recreated.

The Anger of God
Headline pbk £5.99 0747242623

The Assassin's Riddle
Headline pbk £5.99 0747254389

By Murder's Bright Light
Headline pbk £5.99 0747244618

The House of Crows
Headline pbk £5.99 0747249180

The House of the Red Slayer
Headline pbk £5.99 0747238472

Murder Most Holy
Headline pbk £5.99 0747239541

The Nightingale Gallery
Headline pbk £5.99 0747237255

JOHN HARVEY

At first glance the character of Detective Inspector Charlie Resnick - scruffy, jazz-loving, overweight yet strangely attractive to women - might appear to be that of another series detective who is little more than the sum of his idiosyncrasies. It is to John Harvey's credit that Resnick strikes the reader as a far more believable and rounded character than the majority of fictional detectives. Over the course of eight novels Harvey has added substance to his creation, revealing the reasons for his inherent sadness (his wife's desertion), his weight problem (each book contains many recipes for mouth-watering but incredibly fattening sandwiches) and his love of stray cats (substitutes for the children he wanted but never had). Resnick is not the clichéd, maverick cop of so much fiction, scornful and contemptuous of authority, the cop who solves cases by doing it his way. Resnick is a committed team player, depending on his colleagues to complete an investigation. His team is not just a supporting cast but a collection of highly individual and not always attractive characters with their own fully defined prejudices and problems. The covers of the books proclaim 'A Resnick Novel' but the other members of the CID team are vital in driving the plot forward and providing the black humour. The Resnick novels, indeed, are police procedurals without equal in British crime fiction and the setting of Nottingham (a city with its own seamy side) is convincingly and effectively realised.

Cold Light
Mandarin pbk £5.99 074931818X

Cutting Edge
Mandarin pbk £5.99 0749321504

Easy Meat
Mandarin pbk £5.99 0749321326

Living Proof
Mandarin pbk £5.99 0749318236

Off Minor
Mandarin pbk £5.99 0749321555

Rough Treatment
Mandarin pbk £5.99 074932211X

Still Water
Heineman hbk £15.99 0434003263

Wasted Years
Mandarin pbk £5.99 0749318422

VICTOR HEADLEY

In his Yardie trilogy, originally published by a small, independent publisher X-Press and later taken up by Pan, Victor Headley has produced both a convincing account of drug gang rivalries on the streets of north London and exciting and original contributions to black British writing and to the British thriller. His unvarnished, direct stories of the rise and rise of D., from drugs courier on the run to godfather of a drugs empire, make powerful and gripping reading.

Excess
Pan pbk £5.99 0330333127

Fetish
The X-Press pbk £5.99 1874509204

Yardie
Pan pbk £4.99 033033042X

Yush!
Pan pbk £4.99 0330337335

LAUREN HENDERSON

Lauren Henderson is a young London journalist who has, in the last three years, produced, in quick succession, three witty and inventive mysteries set in the capital and featuring her reprobate heroine Sam Jones. Sam, an unusual combination of sculptress and detective, takes time off from working on the silver mobiles she produces in her run-down Holloway warehouse, and from the complications of her love life, to solve mysteries set among the citizens of contemporary London.

The Black Rubber Dress
Hutchinson pbk £9.99 0091801842

Dead White Female
Hodder pbk £5.99 0340649151

Too Many Blondes
Hodder pbk £6.99 0340649178

'Nobody from the Amazing Kingdom bothered to check with previous employers, such as the New York City Police Department, to inquire about allegations of bribery, moral turpitude, substance abuse, witness

CARL HIAASEN

Born and raised in Fort Lauderdale, Florida, Hiaasen worked as a journalist on a number of papers before settling at the *Miami Herald*, where he became an important member of an investigative team covering such topics as corruption and drug smuggling. Together with a colleague, William Montalbano, Hiaasen wrote three novels (*Powder Burn, Trap Line* and *Death in China*). These enjoyable but conventional thrillers were little preparation for the books Hiaasen was to write on his own when the partnership dissolved. Hiaasen's novels are genuinely suspenseful and yet what the reader remembers most from his work are the quirky, distorted scenarios he creates, his ability to take an incident and spin it out to a logical but extreme conclusion, his knack of creating bizarre villains and outlandish heroes. Only in a Carl Hiaasen novel does an ex-investigator dispose of a Mafia hit-man by laying him out with a stuffed marlin head. Only in a Hiaasen novel does a deranged bad guy spend the last half of the book with a dead dog's rotting head firmly embedded by the teeth in his forearm. Only Hiaasen can create, as a hero, an ex-State governor called Skink who has gone native and now lives in the Florida wilds where his favourite meals are roadkill. There is little surprise that P.J. O'Rourke hailed Hiaasen's work as 'better than literature' or, indeed, that the same writer claimed that 'reading Hiaasen will do more to damage the Florida tourist trade than anything except an actual visit to Florida.'

tampering and the unnecessary use of deadly force, to wit, the pistol-whipping of a young man suspected of shoplifting a bag of cheese-flavoured Doritos.'

Carl Hiaasen, Native Tongue

The Carl Hiaasen Omnibus
Picador pbk £9.99 0330336207

Double Whammy
Pan pbk £5.99 0330309870

Native Tongue
Pan pbk £5.99 0330321935

Skin Tight
Pan pbk £5.99 0330314203

Stormy Weather
Pan pbk £5.99 0330340948

Strip Tease
Pan pbk £5.99 0330352075

Tourist Season
Pan pbk £5.99 0330322362

WITH WILLIAM MONTALBANO

A Death in China
Pan pbk £4.99 0330329367

Powder Burn
Pan pbk £5.99 0330326651

Trap Line
Pan pbk £4.99 033032666X

GEORGE V. HIGGINS

Bostonian lawyer George V. Higgins burst on the American crime writing scene with a bang in 1972 when he published The *Friends of Eddie Coyle*, later filmed with Robert Mitchum. Since then he has produced more than twenty books, some of them novels about Washington and the political scene but most of them crime novels set somewhere between Boston's sleazy pool halls and its Halls of Justice. Just as Raymond Chandler created his Los Angeles and Dashiell Hammett his San Francisco, so Higgins has given us his Boston. Presumably in Boston they talk a lot since, in all Higgins's work, the first thing that hits the reader is the strength of the dialogue. Whether snarling from the side of the mouth with only a cigarette butt or mouthful of spit for punctuation, or speaking in the crispest Ivy League accent money can buy, Higgins's characters reveal themselves in conversation. The criminal offering an attorney a bribe, the assistant D.A. in search of a promotion, a mobster telling an assassin to kill an opponent – all these are made memorable through their distinctive speech. Higgins's dialogue is up there with Elmore Leonard's and his characters, from Eddie Coyle to the world-weary Jerry Kennedy, a lawyer who has taken on too many cases of the wrong kind, linger in the mind. Higgins himself is said to dislike the tag of crime writing given to his work. However he is defined, he remains one of the most interesting of contemporary American writers.

Bomber's Law
Warner pbk £5.99 0751508225

The Mandeville Talent
Warner pbk £5.99 0751500550

Outlaws
Warner pbk £4.99 0747409714

Swan Boats at Four
Warner pbk £5.99 0751514659

Trust
Warner pbk £4.50 0747409730

Victories
Warner pbk £4.99 0747409609

Wonderful Years, Wonderful Years
Warner pbk £4.50 0747409749

PATRICIA HIGHSMITH

Graham Greene once stated that Patricia Highsmith was a 'poet of apprehension'. One of the finest female writers within the genre, she is certainly capable of creating characters with a psychological depth which other crime writers find hard to match. Her first novel, Strangers on a Train, remains one of her best known works and this story of a man drawn unwillingly into a bizarre, murder-swapping pact by a chance acquaintance made on a train journey was turned into a memorable Hitchcock film, with a script by Raymond Chandler. In the mid-fifties Highsmith created her most famous character, the anti-hero Tom Ripley, an amoral leisure-loving amateur villain resident in France, who is capable of the most ruthless crimes, up to and including murder, if his own interests are threatened. After the first Ripley novel, The Talented Mr. Ripley, the character appeared in a number further books, in each one demonstrating his determination to allow nothing and nobody to stand in the way of his aspirations and objectives. In her later books Highsmith changed her focus from actual, physical crimes to spiritual angst and mental cruelty but continued to write in a spare, pared-down style that heightened the already chilling quality of her stories. Few crime writers have been so adept at entering the psyches of their characters and few have succeeded in creating, as she did, a world of her own which, as Graham Greene also remarked, is 'more frighteningly real than the house next door.'

The Blunderer
Penguin pbk £5.99 0140101160

The Boy Who Followed Ripley
Penguin pbk £5.99 0140057390

The Cry of the Owl
Penguin pbk £5.99 0140036040

Deep Water
Penguin pbk £5.99 0140038582

A Dog's Ransom
Penguin pbk £4.99 0140039449

Edith's Diary
Penguin pbk £5.99 0140048022

Eleven
Penguin pbk £4.99 0140034714

Found in the Street
Penguin pbk £5.99 0140097783

Game for the Living
Penguin pbk £4.99 0140101187

The Glass Cell
Penguin pbk £4.99 0140036032

People Who Knock on the Door
Penguin pbk £5.99 0140067418

The Ripley Omnibus
Penguin pbk £10.99 014017236X

Ripley Under Ground
Penguin pbk £5.99 0140036024

Ripley Under Water
Penguin pbk £5.99 0140159525

Ripley's Game
Penguin pbk £5.99 0140037780

Strangers on a Train
Penguin pbk £5.99 0140037969

A Suspension of Mercy
Penguin pbk £5.99 0140034706

The Talented Mr Ripley
Penguin pbk £5.99 014004020X

This Sweet Sickness
pbk £4.99 0140034692

The Tremor of Forgery
Penguin pbk £4.99 0140101152

The Two Faces of January
Penguin pbk £5.99 0140101179

REGINALD HILL

The strength of the British crime novel for many years has been the traditional story in which the reader knows that the cerebral detective will triumph and the natural order of things will reassert itself. Few of the novels in this tradition traffic in ambiguity or ambivalence. Reginald Hill is one of a handful of British crime writers who has succeeded in creating stories that have the originality and ingenuity of the classics of the genre but which also show the complexities of moral and social issues in modern life. Hill's first book *A Clubbable Woman*, published in 1970, introduced the two mainstays of his novels - the rude, aggressive but shrewd Superintendent Andy Dalziel and the intelligent and sensitive Chief Inspector Peter Pascoe, both from Mid Yorkshire's CID. Each successive book in the series has been an entertaining, humorous and sophisticated exercise in traditional storytelling, notable also for its deft characterization and pertinent social commentary. Unlike the characters in many crime series all the people in Hill's novels are changed by the crimes in which they are involved. Even the phlegmatic Sergeant Wield and the hard Dalziel experience emotions which alter their beliefs and understanding. The novels are set in the Rotary clubs, colleges, rugby clubs and amateur dramatic societies of Mid Yorkshire and Hill is skilful both at celebrating the worth of such social groups and institutions while revealing the frailties and darker emotions of the people who constitute them. His books are not afraid to tackle powerful issues - pornography, animal rights, the miners' strike - but these emerge naturally from the story he is telling. Reginald Hill has recently been given the CWA Cartier Diamond Dagger Award for a lifetime's contribution to the crime novel, an accolade that this master of the genre thoroughly deserved.

An Advancement of Learning
HarperCollins pbk £4.99
0006498590

An April Shroud
HarperCollins pbk £5.99
0006498604

Asking for the Moon
HarperCollins pbk £5.99
0006479340

Blood Sympathy
HarperCollins pbk £4.99
0586218513

Bones and Silence
HarperCollins pbk £4.99
0586211284

Born Guilty
HarperCollins pbk £4.99
0586218521

Child's Play
HarperCollins pbk £4.99
0586072578

A Clubbable Woman
HarperCollins pbk £4.99
0006498612

Deadheads
HarperCollins pbk £5.99
0006499910

Death of A Dormouse
HarperCollins pbk £4.99
0586205462

Exit Lines
HarperCollins pbk £5.99
0006510337

A Killing Kindness
HarperCollins pbk £5.99
0006499899

Pictures of Perfection
HarperCollins pbk £5.99
0006490115

A Pinch of Snuff
HarperCollins pbk £4.99
0586072500

Recalled to Life
HarperCollins pbk £4.99
0586217320

A Ruling Passion
HarperCollins pbk £5.99
0006499902

Underworld
HarperCollins pbk £4.99
0586204520

The Wood Beyond
HarperCollins pbk £5.99
0006479944

TONY HILLERMAN

The stories of Tony Hillerman take their readers to the canyons and mesas of the Land Between the Secret Mountains and immerse them in the traditions and lore of the Navajo people. A former wire-service reporter and college professor, Hillerman has created a thoroughly original and convincing pair of Navajo Tribal Policemen in Jim Chee and Joe Leaphorn. Leaphorn, the older of the two, respects the ways of the elders but is sceptical about what he regards as sorcery and witchcraft. Chee, on the other hand, is a young shaman trained to return the Navajo to the path of beauty and harmony through ceremonies involving sacred singing, sweat lodges and sandpaintings. The early Hillerman novels feature one or other of the Tribal Policemen but in *Skinwalkers* the two came together and they have remained together in the novels since. Hillerman's elegantly written stories, with their hauntingly beautiful sense of place, are amongst the most original of contemporary crime novels. Their recreation of a society with very different values to those of the larger society surrounding it, one in which detection and deduction take a very different path, is wholly convincing and engrossing.

Coyote Waits
Penguin pbk £5.99 0140177310

The Leaphorn Mysteries
Penguin pbk £8.99 0140177329

People of Darkness
Warner pbk £4.99 0751502464

Skinwalkers
Penguin pbk £5.99 0140177299

Talking God
Penguin pbk £5.99 0140177302

A Thief of Time
Penguin pbk £5.99 0140177280

CHESTER HIMES (1909 - 1984)

As a black American in the thirties Himes knew what it was to be an outsider. Indeed he began writing during a period in jail for armed robbery. Frequently described as the first black American crime writer, he was, for much of his life, largely ignored in his homeland and lived and worked first in France and then in Spain where he died in 1984. Despite his long exile, Himes's acute memories of his early experiences and his lively imagination served him well as a writer. His greatest books – what he called his 'domestic thrillers' – are best known now as the Harlem Cycle. These marvellously lucid and darkly humorous tales of murder and larceny in the streets of Harlem are unrivalled in their ability to convey the atmosphere of a black, urban community. A few saints and a lot of sinners inhabit Himes's Harlem, all loosely policed by Coffin Ed Johnson and Gravedigger Jones, the hardest and meanest cops on the street. 'They had to be tough to work in Harlem. Colored folks didn't respect colored cops but they respected big, shiny pistols and sudden death.'(A Rage in Harlem) Himes pulled few punches. The Harlem Cycle is hilarious and tragic, filled with sharp, quick-witted dialogue and a genuine sense of the temptations, the danger and the violence of the streets. Himes's influence has been significant and he can now be recognised as one of the major American crime writers.

The Harlem Cycle Volume 1 *A Rage in Harlem, The Real Cool Killers, The Crazy Kill*
Payback Press pbk £7.99 0862415969

The Harlem Cycle Volume 2 *The Big Gold Dream, All Shot Up, The Heat's On*
Payback Press pbk £7.99 0862416310

The Harlem Cycle Volume 3
Cotton Comes to Harlem, Blind Man With a Pistol, Plan B
Payback Press pbk £7.99 0862416922

If He Hollers Let Him Go
Serpent's Tail pbk £8.99 1852422335

PAGING MR HIMES
by James Sallis

The author of the dazzling Lew Griffin novels writes about a novelist he admires profoundly, the author of 'one of America's scant handful of perfect novels.'

When first I began writing about Chester Himes, some twenty years ago, every one of his books was out of print here in the States. When he was known at all, he was known for the series of detective novels that included *Cotton Comes to Harlem*, eight books often perceived as cynical potboilers, sellouts, rags and bones from a once promising, 'literary' novelist. Meanwhile, works such as *If He Hollers Let Him Go, Cast the First Stone, Run Man Run* and his central masterpiece, *The Primitive*, one of America's scant handful of perfect novels, seemed, if not lost, then terminally misplaced. But these books would not go away. They would not be (in Sartre's phrase) gagged by the silence of others. They would not get out of America's face. Every five or six years they'd stutter back into print. Obviously something in Himes' work went on connecting in a very real, very enduring way with readers – readers who had witnessed civil rights and black power movements of the sixties, pehaps; readers who remember the Watts riots and Rodney King; readers who wonder just how today's inner-city apartheid, this partitioning of a nation, came about. Finally now, readers and critics are catching up. Today all of Chester Himes' books are back in print. James Lundquist's and Stephen Milliken's admirable early studies have been joined by Robert Skinner's *Two Guns from Harlem*, Michel Fabre's and Skinner's *Conversations with Chester Himes* and a recent biography from Fabre and Edward Margolies. Himes is also featured in, indeed central to, a major new study of African-American mysteries, *The Blues Detective*. Increasingly readers and critics recognize that it's not with Richard Wright or James Baldwin – both securely within the naturalist, European style, both embraced by the academic canon – that we find our surest route to the black experience and contemporary black writing, but with Chester Himes. The fantastical, poetic structure of *The Primitive*, the expressionist grotesques and hyperboles of the Harlem cycle, at once look back to African story-telling forms and forward to contemporary literary forms. Chester Himes is not only a major American writer; he is our central American black writer.

Himes was born in Jefferson City, Missouri, 1909, to a light-skinned, elitist mother and dark-skinned, bandy-legged father who taught blacksmithing and other commercial arts at Negro technical colleges. Over the years the rift between his parents grew unbreachable. Giving up on high expectations she'd had for his father, mother Estelle seems to have transferred those expectations, and ultimately her profound disappointment as well, to Chester. But Chester could never fit himself to anyone's expectations: his mother's, the university's, the literary establishment's, even his own. At Ohio State he joined the black fraternity and tooled about town and campus in raccoon coat and roadster. Soon, though, he was spending time in Cleveland's game and sporting houses. Soon, too, with the kind of reckless, irrational behavior that became a virtual leimotif in his life, Himes tried to dovetail his two worlds. Taking a group of students to one of his regular haunts, he professes incredulity that both worlds should turn against him, and that subsequently he should be expelled.

Himes fell to running errands and interference for gamblers and hustlers. He also worked various Cleveland hotels as a bellhop; at one of these he plunged forty feet down an open elevator shaft. Recovery was slow, resumption of old habits following recovery almost immediate. A number of skirmishes with the law led finally to a sentence for armed robbery. Himes entered prison at age nineteen. It was there that he began to write. Stories appeared in black newspapers, then, with only his prison number as byline, in *Esquire*. His first novels, *If He Hollers Let Him Go*, *Lonely Crusade* and to an extent *The Third Generation*, were protest novels somewhat in the manner of Richard Wright and others. From the first, though, there were significant differences that set Himes' work apart.

Thematically, for one thing, he wrote of middle class, educated blacks. No Bigger Thomases here. For another, he was a highly original writer, spinning out scenes we've never read before, taking close notice of the world from perspectives rarely encountered, convincing us with the sheer physicality of his writing. Himes' novels were also tightly structured, *If He Hollers* around a series of reflective, ever-mutable dreams, *Lonely Crusade* around a series of philosophical dialogues. Exam question: Choose one word to describe Himes' work.

Answer: Intensity. A book like *The Primitive* immerses us so fully in the experiences of its characters that our reaction to the book becomes an almost physical one. For this intensity and informing structure, as well as for his addressing of our most profound social problems, the writer with whom Himes has most in common, it seems to me, is Nathanael West, whose *Miss Lonelyhearts* is another of America's undervalued, almost perfect novels.

The detective novels for which he's best known came about with Himes' relocation to Paris. *Lonely Crusade* had met with a poor reception in the States and newer manuscripts wandered New York streets like the popular folk song's boll weevil, just lookin' for a home, while in France Gallimard had published him to great acclaim. Fleeing America's racism, Himes joined a select group of black expatriates. At Gallimard editor Marcel Duhamel's suggestion, Himes wrote his first mystery, which promptly won 1958's Grand Prix de Litterature Policière. The specific genius of these books is hard to define. They began, inasmuch as Himes understood the form, as fairly standard thrillers. But, again, Himes could never live up to expectations. He could never say what he was supposed to; he was compelled to say something else. He'd always been an intuitive writer, burrowing his way to the heart of the matter by feeling alone, by sheer force of will and hard work, by instinct. It would be the same with his detective novels. Improvising like a jazz musician, never knowing from page to page what would happen, he wrote one, then another. Good tunes, solid beat, something you could build on. Precisely what he did. We're coming to recognise now that crime novels provide *the* urban fiction. Few suspected this at the time the Harlem cycle came out – few but Chester Himes. In these books Himes found what artist Odilon Redon called a visual logic for the imagination: figures that could bear the weight of his preoccupations with social and racial problems without toppling beneath that weight, a freedom of form allowing him to recreate his own complex vision of America, of its disenfranchised, its disadvantaged and mortally wounded, unencumbered by intellectual baggage or the demands of naturalism. Chester Himes didn't transcend the genre so much as he personally reinvented it – as, if our fiction is to have any purchase, must all of us. There's nothing else like these books. Nothing. Nowadays, finally, people are reading up and down the twenty-five-year line of Chester Himes' work. Backwards from *Blind Man With a Pistol* to *If He Hollers Let Him Go*. Forwards from *Lonely Crusade* to *A Rage in Harlem* . Rediscovering Chester Himes in all his complexity, all his unity, all his strength and peculiar weaknesses, all his intensity. Recent critical and popular fashion leans heavily on crutches of simile. Often it seems we care less what a thing is than what kind of thing it is. Books sell because they're like the author's last, new movies are touted as six parts this, half a dozen parts that. American literary history offers few analogs to Chester Himes. Nathanael West I've already mentioned. James M. Cain, a writer at least as fundamental to our literature as Hemingway and Fitzgerald, might prove another. Then there are writers like Jim Thompson, Horace McCoy, Philip Wylie, Theodore Sturgeon, Samuel R. Delany. All of them stand apart, having created something the world had never seen before. This may be the highest praise possible. I suppose it might just as well be taken to certify the peripheral nature of these writers, to underline their outlaw status, but (invoking simile myself) I think of jazz, where just such innovations, just such extensions of tradition, initially rejected, became central. Reflecting his family's upheavals, giving voice to his own growing frustration and bitterness, Chester Himes' view of the black American experience was a grim one. In 1966, addressing an audience at the University of Chicago on 'The Dilemma of the Negro Writer in the United States,' Himes noted: 'If this plumbing for the truth reveals within the Negro personality homicidal mania, lust for white women, a pathetic sense of inferiority, paradoxical anti-Semitism, arrogance, Uncle Tomism, hate and fear and self-hate, this then is the effect of oppression on the human personality. These are the daily horrors, the daily realities, the daily experiences of an oppressed minority.' Elsewhere, though, sounding remarkably like one of his models, Faulkner, Himes asserted:

'There is an indomitable quality within the human spirit that can not be destroyed; a face deep within the human personality that is impregnable to all assaults . . . we would be drooling idiots, dangerous maniacs, raving beasts – if it were not for that quality and force within all humans that cries 'I will live.' Chester Himes could never say what others expected him to say. It was not the fashion in his day to refuse to dissemble, to point unflinchingly at the situation of blacks in America, demanding response; not the fashion to tell wild, high tales, to insist that raids on Senegambian villages and the Watts riots, the drums of Congo Square and the higher reaches of African-American literature were points on a line. Perhaps now, in our day, it's time at last to listen to what Chester Himes said.

James Sallis is currently writing a biography of Chester Himes which Payback Press will publish in 1998.

WILLIAM HJORSTBERG

One of the lesser known postwar American fabulists, Hjorstberg
has a great ability to toy playfully with the boundaries of crime
fiction, while demonstrating respect for the conventions of the
genre. His key work is the magnificent *Falling Angel*, memorably
filmed by Alan Parker as *Angel Heart* in 1987. Arguably one of
the finest crime novels of the last twenty five years, *Falling Angel*
is the story of Harry Angel, a classic hard-boiled, slightly seedy
hero, operating in a fifties New York that Hjorstberg richly
evokes in his prose. Arcane clues to help the reader solve
Angel's case are present from the first line yet even the most
jaded devotee of crime fiction is likely to be astonished by the
denouement. *Falling Angel* is a novel which trespasses reward-
ingly on the territory of other genres while remaining a perfect
example of what a noir novel should be. Hjorstberg's most
recent book is *Nevermore*, a lighter work in which Conan Doyle
and Harry Houdini are joined by Edgar Allan Poe in an attempt
to solve a series of murders that echo the latter's stories.
Hjorstberg is an important, readable writer who deserves to be
elevated beyond his current cult status.

Falling Angel
No Exit Press pbk £6.99 1874061599

Nevermore
Orion pbk £5.99 1857994450

CRAIG HOLDEN

In the space of just two novels Craig Holden has burst dramatically on to the US crime writing scene. *The River Sorrow*, his first book, is a chilling tale of a doctor and former junkie, whose grim past lies buried, but not dead, and surfaces, in true noir fashion, to reclaim him. Once his twin obsessions were Denise, a beautiful addict, and heroin itself, both equally seductive and deadly. Now they seem to have returned to haunt him - one in the shape of Storm, a lovely and familiar looking woman, the other in a new and potent synthetic opiate which is likely to prove fatal. James Ellroy said of this novel, 'This is a book that oozes power.' And he should know. Holden's second book, *The Last Sanctuary*, is another triumph. It kicks off with a quintessentially noir opening. Joe Curtis, a Gulf War veteran, is hitching to Seattle to retrieve his errant brother Terry when he stops to accept a lift from a young couple. Once in the car, his worst nightmare begins. In no time he is wanted for robbery and murder, framed by the couple who are members of a bizarre religious cult. As a nationwide manhunt for Joe gets under way, his flight takes him across the US and leads him eventually to the wintry wilds of Alaska where the cult are headed to find their final sanctuary. At the novel's climax, Federal agents, cult members, Canadian Mounties and private detectives are all embroiled in a desperate fight to save Joe or capture him, dead or alive. In only two books Holden has tapped into the beleaguered psyche of America and transformed what he's seen into powerful fiction.

The Last Sanctuary
Pan pbk £5.99 0330349341

The River Sorrow
- Pan pbk £5.99 0330335170

E.W. HORNUNG (1866-1921)

The brother-in-law of Conan Doyle, Hornung is remembered for the creation of the elegant, cricket-playing gentleman-burglar Raffles who, although not rivalling the popularity of Doyle's creations, has also been frequently portrayed on stage and film. Rooted very much in the Edwardian era in which they were written, the stories of Raffles and his faithful friend Bunny retain a period charm that continues to make them readable.

The Collected Raffles Stories
Oxford UP pbk £5.99 0192823248

'A fat man? I didn't see any fat man.'

Michael Innes, *Operation Pax*

ICEBERG SLIM

Robert Beck, aka Iceberg Slim, spent his young adulthood as a pimp, hustler and pusher on the streets of Chicago in the forties and fifties. He witnessed most of the people close to him live miserable, drug-fuelled and crime-driven lives and die early and violent deaths in the ghetto. Yet, after a third horrendous stretch in jail, he emerged with the strength to turn his life around and to use his experiences on the streets to become a writer. The seven powerful books that followed speak with the raw dialect of a dark underworld of sex, misogyny, booze, dope and crime. The writing is clever as well as bleak and uncompromising. Iceberg Slim tells it how it is and his hard-hitting, tough-talking street prose is as real today as it was thirty years ago. He has long been a cult writer and the example of an extremely intelligent individual who used his wits and intuition to stay alive in the depths of a dog-eat-dog environment has been an inspiring one. His influence on black writing and on eighties rap music and nineties gangsta rap has been immense.

Airtight Willie and Me
Payback Press pbk £5.99
0862416965

Long White Con
Payback Press pbk £5.99
0862416949

Mama Black Widow
Payback Press pbk £5.99
0862416329

Trick Baby
Payback Press pbk £5.99
0862415942

MICHAEL INNES

Under his own name J. I. M. Stewart wrote a number of non-genre novels and critical studies of Kipling, Hardy and Joyce amongst others. Under the pseudonym of Michael Innes he published, over a period of more than half a century, a succession of examples of what Julian Symons once called the 'farceur' school of detective fiction. Beginning with *Death at the President's Lodging*, in 1936, these are donnish stories, filled with literary allusions and quotations, which feature the stolid police inspector, John Appleby. Self-consciously literary, often whimsical, they are not to everyone's taste but Innes's work is urbanely well-written and represents probably the best example of an important strand in traditional British crime fiction.

Appleby's Answer
Gollancz pbk £4.99 0575056363

Death at the President's Lodging
Penguin pbk £5.99 0140105557

From London Far
Penguin pbk £5.99 0140172416

Hare Sitting Up
Gollancz pbk £4.99 0575052104

The New Sonia Wayward
Gollancz pbk £4.99 0575046341

Operation Pax
Penguin pbk £5.99 0140115161

The Secret Vanguard
Gollancz pbk £4.99 0575057106

Silence Observed
Gollancz pbk £3.99 057505381X

ELIZABETH IRONSIDE

Elizabeth Ironside is a widely travelled author, currently resident in Tel Aviv. Her first book won the John Creasey Award for Best First Crime Novel and her second was shortlisted for the prestigious CWA Gold Dagger Award. Her most recent book *The Accomplice* is a polished investigation into the personality of an apparently ordinary Englishwoman whose mysterious past amid the terrors and betrayals of Eastern Europe in 1945 is slowly revealed.

A Very Private Enterprise
Hodder pbk £5.99 0340640332
The Accomplice
Hodder pbk £5.99 0340640375
Death in the Garden
Hodder pbk £5.99 0340640359

EUGENE IZZI

Chicago-born Izzi is the critically-acclaimed author of a dozen crime novels, all set in his home town and each one a gripping read. Unusually he makes no use of a detective in his books, no central character whose presence dominates the books. Instead the books are peopled by characters who drift from one side of the law to another, characters who move through the streets and alleys of the Windy City, just trying and, sometimes, failing to stay alive. In some ways he represents a rougher version of George V. Higgins, with the smoothness of the latter's Boston replaced by Chicago grit. Certainly he matches Higgins in his use of dialogue. All his books are worthy of attention but *Tribal Secrets*, with a familiar Izzi theme of a man trying unsuccessfully to escape his past, is as good a starting point as any.

Bulletin from the Street
Arrow pbk £5.99 0099208415
Players
Arrow pbk £5.99 0099208717
Safe Harbour
Arrow pbk £5.99 0099208512
Tribal Secrets
Arrow pbk £4.99 009920861X

BILL JAMES

Belonging to what one might call the 'dirty realism' school of crime fiction, British author Bill James has written a number of novels featuring Colin Harpur and Francis Iles, the one Chief Superintendent and a hardened copper, the other a faintly smarmy Acting Deputy Chief Constable. Harpur is an excellent character but all of the police in these books are splendidly realistic, operating convincingly in that endless grey area of the law where the line between crooks and coppers fades, slowly at first, and then only too quickly. Paradoxically, for a thoroughly British series, the novels have a strong American feel, perhaps because they possess more honesty than many of their peers. Harpur, for instance, stuck in a dreary marriage, quite calculatedly has an affair with a married woman, even though (or because) she happens to be another officer's wife. This is no Inspector Morse. Set mostly in Wales and the South West, the books have an agreeably downbeat humour and are enlivened by flashes of violence that are entirely credible. They make up an underrated series and one that's definitely worth investigating.

Astride a Grave
Pan pbk £4.50 0330321749

Club
Pan pbk £4.50 0330323830

The Detective Is Dead
Pan pbk £4.99 033034854X

Harpur & Iles : An Omnibus
Pan pbk £6.99 0330332864

In Good Hands
Pan pbk £4.99 0330342967

Protection
Pan pbk £5.99 0330348949

Roses, Roses
Pan pbk £4.99 0330338498

Take
Pan pbk £3.99 0330316222

Top Banana
Pan pbk £5.99 0330350080

P.D. JAMES

Aficionados of the classic English detective story have come to expect that the traditional virtues of the genre – strong plot, credible detection, memorable, occasionally eccentric characters – will be upheld in the work of P. D. James. In many ways P. D. James has brought the 'educated' crime story once practised by Dorothy L. Sayers and Margery Allingham into the modern age and given it, if not necessarily a greater sophistication (her predecessors were sophisticated writers), then certainly a much greater level of realism. Her books feature, separately, two central characters. Adam Dalgleish, played by Roy Marsden in several TV versions of James stories, is a sensitive combination of published poet and high-flying police officer. The books in which he appears are often complex and intelligent examinations of crimes committed within bastions of upper middle class life and culture – literary publishing, for example, in *Original Sin* or the legal world of the Middle Temple in P. D. James's most recent novel, *A Certain Justice.* Cordelia Gray, who appears in fewer books than Dalgleish, is, in many ways, a more interesting character. A spirited female detective, who approaches each case with a refreshingly detached eye, she is one of the most engaging heroines in contemporary British crime fiction. In all her books P. D. James has shown her skill as a narrator of exciting and suspenseful stories which sacrifice nothing in the way of intelligence and style.

The Black Tower
Penguin pbk £4.99 0140129553

Cover Her Face
Penguin pbk £4.99 0140129588

A Dalgleish Trilogy
Penguin pbk £9.99 0140159541

Death of an Expert Witness
Penguin pbk £4.99 0140129561

Devices and Desires
Penguin pbk £5.99 0140132910

Innocent Blood
Penguin pbk £5.99 0140129596

A Mind to Murder
Penguin pbk £4.99 0140038507

Original Sin
Penguin pbk £5.99 0140245510

A Second Dalgleish Trilogy
Penguin pbk £9.99 0140232885

Shroud for a Nightingale
Penguin pbk £4.99 0140129537

The Skull Beneath the Skin
Penguin pbk £4.99 014012960X

A Taste for Death
Penguin pbk £5.99 0140129545

Trilogy of Death
Penguin pbk £9.99 0140173900

Unnatural Causes
Penguin pbk £4.99 0140129618

An Unsuitable Job for a Woman
Penguin pbk £4.99 014012957X

SEBASTIEN JAPRISOT

Dislocated identity is a recurring theme in his work and so it seems apt that Sebastien Japrisot is the anagrammatic pseudonym of Jean-Baptiste Rossi who published his first novel at the age of seventeen and went on to translate Salinger to much acclaim in France. The first Japrisot mysteries appeared in the mid-sixties and are reflective of the French cultural landscape at that time. Japrisot employs the cool, image-free narrative techniques of the *nouveau roman* to weave sly, amoral tales of escape and fractured personality reminiscent of the films of Truffaut or Godard. *10.30 from Marseilles* gives a modern twist to the 'body on a train' formula, whilst in *Trap for Cinderella* and *The Lady in the Car with Glasses and a Gun* (perhaps the typical Japrisot novel) young women are forced to reconstruct their identities in different but equally baffling and suspenseful situations. Japrisot later expanded the *cherchez la femme* device with the labyrinthine and erotic *Women in Evidence*. Most recently Japrisot abandoned the mystery genre with *A Very Long Engagement*, a compassionate and moving account of the Great War that could be described as a French conterpart to Sebastian Faulks's *Birdsong*.

The works of Sebastien Japrisot are currently out of print in this country. Harvil Press plan to re-publish some of his novels in 1998.

QUINTIN JARDINE

Quintin Jardine has worked in journalism and PR and has published six novels featuring the tough, high-flying Edinburgh police chief Bob Skinner. These have been much praised not only for their assured plotting and readability but for their succcessful evocation of a Scotland and an Edinburgh that the tourists don't see.

Skinner's Festival
Headline pbk £5.99 0747241406

Skinner's Mission
Headline hbk £16.99 0747214662

Skinner's Ordeal
Headline pbk £5.99 0747250421

Skinner's Round
Headline pbk £5.99 0747250413

Skinner's Rules
Headline pbk £5.99 0747241392

Skinner's Trail
Headline pbk £5.99 0747241414

'Oh, I feel that if a man had sufficient violence in him to slit his own throat, he's certainly capable of slitting another's.'

P. D. James,
A Taste for Death

MICHAEL JECKS

Michael Jecks gave up a career in the computer industry to concentrate on his fiction and on the study of medieval history. He has published several historical mysteries, set in the West Country in the fourteenth century, which feature Sir Baldwin Furnshill, Keeper of the King's Peace, and his friend, the bailiff of Lydford Castle, Simon Puttock. These are entertaining and well-researched excursions into a period that is popular with fans of the historical crime story.

The Crediton Killings
Headline hbk £17.99 0747218811

The Last Templar
Headline pbk £5.99 0747250618

The Merchant's Partner
Headline pbk £5.99 0747250707

A Moorland Hanging
Headline pbk £5.99 0747250715

DAN KAVANAGH

One wouldn't have to be much of a detective, private or otherwise, to discover the alter ego of Dan Kavanagh. In the early eighties, before fame and dreams of Booker prize triumphs came his way, fledgeling novelist Julian Barnes dashed off a handful of crime novels featuring Nick Duffy - a bisexual private eye and ex-copper known to friend and foe alike as just Duffy. Duffy himself is an inspired creation but the creation of Kavanagh was even more inspired, for it freed Barnes from his more literary constraints and allowed him to pursue a more earthy and humorous course. Certainly the Duffy novels are in a (perhaps lower) class of their own - vicious, seedy and frequently hilarious. The nearest rivals they have are the London noir novels of the late Derek Raymond and they are, like Raymond's books, amongst the earliest hard-boiled crime books in the UK. Duffy himself is a superb character and entirely at home in the dingy demi-monde of the London streets with its barrow boy villains, cheerful tarts and general Sweeney-like atmosphere. Aided by Carol, his long-suffering partner (and, in a novel twist, a WPC) Duffy, beaten, bedraggled and abused, always comes up trumps in the end. After four Duffy books, Kavanagh went AWOL and Barnes sat down and wrote *The History of the World in Ten and a Half Chapters*. The rest is history. Let's hope, however, that Kavanagh and Duffy are simply on the back-burner, having a breather, before they step out and about once more.

Duffy Omnibus
Penguin pbk £9.99 0140158243

H.R.F. KEATING

Best known for the series of ingenious and amusing novels featuring the Bombay police inspector Ganesh Ghote (many of which are currently unavailable), Keating has been a prolific writer of carefully-constructed mysteries and some of his most satisfying work has been set outside the series. He was for a long time the crime fiction reviewer of *The Times* and has also written a useful manual for aspiring crime writers.

The Bad Detective
Pan pbk £4.99 033034403X
Doing Wrong
Pan pbk £4.99 0330340042
The Good Detective
Pan pbk £4.99 0330343556
The Inspector Ghote Mysteries
(Contains *The Perfect Murder,
Inspector Ghote's Good Crusade*
and *Inspector Ghote Caught in
Meshes*)
Pan pbk £8.99 0330348566
The Rich Detective
Pan pbk £4.99 0330332988
Writing Crime Fiction
A & C Black pbk £7.99
0713639210

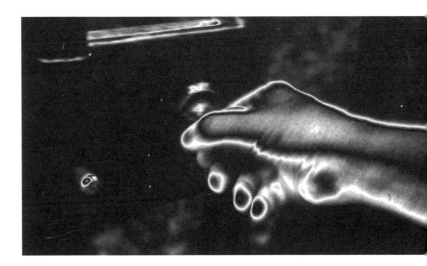

FAYE KELLERMAN

The wife of crime novelist Jonathan, Faye Kellerman is a skilled writer of taut and exciting crime thrillers in her own right. Her work is made particularly distinctive by the way that, through the central partnership in her books, that of Pete Decker and Rina Lazarus, she can examine both the rituals, beliefs and laws of Judaism and the gritty realities of life as an LAPD detective. Kellerman's emphasis on moral and religious laws as much as the laws of the constitution throws new light on the classic plot-driven detective story and raise interesting issues of guilt, justice and responsibility. Her novels are also underpinned by themes of identity and displacement in modern society and by the moral dilemmas faced by many in multi-racial America. From the awful events of violation in *The Ritual Bath* to kidnapping in *Grievous Sin* and mass murder in *Serpent's Tooth*, Kellerman tackles the worst of crimes and, through her keen eye for the detail of police work and her gift for creating strong characters, produces engrossing and satisfying fiction.

Day of Atonement
Headline pbk £5.99 0747234310

False Prophet
Headline pbk £5.99 074723955X

Grievous Sin
Headline pbk £5.99 074724118X

Justice
Headline pbk £5.99 0747249490

Milk and Honey
Headline pbk £5.99 0747234302

Prayers for the Dead
Headline pbk £5.99 0747252319

Sacred and Profane
Headline pbk £5.99 0747242992

Sanctuary
Headline pbk £5.99 0747247021

Serpant's Tooth
Headline hbk £16.99 0747216053

JONATHAN KELLERMAN

Jonathan Kellerman lives in California with his wife and fellow crime writer, Faye Kellerman. A former child psychologist, Kellerman artfully combines detective fiction with the insights into the workings of the human mind that his training and earlier career gave him. Kellerman's hero is not a cop but an academic – Dr Alex Delaware, a psychologist whose theoretical investigations regularly lead to real crimes and real murders. Delaware is an unusually domesticated hero by the standards of most crime fiction. He has a live-in girlfriend and a pet dog to come home to; he is thoughtful and, as far as possible, non-violent, more likely to indulge in psychological profiling than fisticuffs. Yet Kellerman is not afraid to lift the lid on California cool and reveal some brutal stories and sick minds. His stylish and often dark thrillers embrace many modern fears and preoccupations, from serial killers to child abuse, and Delaware's intelligent investigations expose the betrayals, cruelties and wrecked lives that can co-exist with the style and sunshine of the West Coast.

Bad Love
Warner pbk £5.99 0751508497

Blood Test
Warner pbk £5.99 075150727X

The Butcher's Theatre
Warner pbk £6.99 0751502316

The Clinic
Warner pbk £5.99 0751518891

Devil's Waltz
Warner pbk £6.99 0751501085

Over the Edge
Warner pbk £5.99 0751505900

Private Eyes
Warner pbk £6.99 0751500208

Self-Defence
Warner pbk £6.99 0751512184

Silent Partner
Warner pbk £5.99 0751510653

Time Bomb
Warner pbk £5.99 0751512702

The Web
Warner pbk £5.99 075151585X

When the Bough Breaks
Warner pbk £5.99 0751506761

KAREN KIJEWSKI

In the wake of the success of authors such as Sue Grafton and Sara Paretsky have come shelves of crime books featuring feisty, wisecracking female private eyes. Few are as successful in their own right as Karen Kijewski's series of books about Kat Colorado. Since the first, *Katwalk*, was published in 1989 and was immediately showered with awards in the US, Kijewski has produced another seven of these hugely enjoyable books which have a genuinely different and engaging heroine in Colorado.

Alley Kat Blues
Headline pbk £5.99 0747248389

Copy Kat
Headline pbk £4.99 0747241775

Honky Tonk Kat
Headline pbk £5.99 0747254745

Kat Scratch Fever
Headline hbk £17.99 0747217890

Katapult
Headline pbk £5.99 0747243085

Kat's Cradle
Headline pbk £4.99 0747243093

Katwalk
Headline pbk £4.99 0747242119

Wild Kat
Headline pbk £5.99 0747245835

PHILIP KERR

One of Britain's most successful crime and thriller writers, Kerr has had a career sharply divided in two. His first three novels, known collectively as the *Berlin Noir Trilogy,* are a brilliant blend of history and crime fiction. *March Violets* and *The Pale Criminal* are both set in Berlin just prior to World War II and feature Bernie Gunther, private investigator and former member of KRIPO, the German secret police. Backed by meticulous research, Kerr successfully transposes the classic Chandler / Hammett novels to the very mean streets of Nazi-infested Berlin. The third novel, *A German Requiem,* sees Gunther leaving Berlin after the war to track down a former KRIPO colleague in Vienna. Soon the icy winds of the Cold War are blowing down Gunther's neck. After writing these excellent and original books, Kerr performed a huge volte-face and went on to produce a number of very different books. Set in the near future, his next few novels could be termed 'techno-thrillers' and have been snapped up by Hollywood, although, as yet, no film versions have appeared. Probably written with more than half an eye on potential film producers, these slick, extremely intelligent thrillers have earned Kerr a reputation as England's answer to Michael Crichton. By swapping detectives and lugers for scientists and stunguns, Kerr has thrust his novels into the twenty-first century and gained a larger readership, but crime aficionados can be forgiven for mourning the loss of Bernie Gunther.

Berlin Noir
Penguin pbk £9.99 0140231706

Dead Meat
Arrow pbk £5.99 009977271X

Esau
Arrow pbk £5.99 0099508419

A German Requiem
Penguin pbk £5.99 0140139958

Gridiron
Vintage pbk £5.99 0099594315

March Violets
Penguin pbk £5.99 0140114661

The Pale Criminal
Penguin pbk £5.99 014011467X

A Philosophical Investigation
Arrow pbk £5.99 0099736411

LAURIE KING

Laurie King won the John Creasey Award for Best First Crime Novel and the equivalent Edgar award in the USA when she published her first book. The only other writer to pull off this prestigious double has been Patricia Cornwell. Since winning the awards King has published a further two novels featuring the San Francisco homicide detectives Martinelli and Hawkin. She has also begun an intriguing and very different series, set in 1914, in which an intelligent teenage girl is apprenticed to a retired Sherlock Holmes.

A Grave Talent
HarperCollins pbk £4.99
0006493548

A Monstrous Regiment of Women
HarperCollins hbk £15.99
0002326108

To Play the Fool
HarperCollins pbk £5.99
0006493556

With Child
HarperCollins pbk £8.99
0002326361

JOE LANSDALE

Joe Lansdale is one of the new stars of American crime fiction. His stylish mix of high farce and relentless violence and action comes together with the inspired male bonding between his two central characters Hap Collins and Leonard Pine, to form some of the most enjoyable tall stories in the genre. Lansdale is an experienced writer who, in the States, has published short story collections with such memorable titles as *Bestsellers Guaranteed* and *Stories by Mama Lansdale's Youngest Boy*. He has also written widely in the horror genre and has won three Bram Stoker Awards from the Horror Writers of America. However, in this country, it is the novels featuring Hap and Leonard which are winning him a growing readership. Hap, white and straight, and Leonard, black and gay, form an odd crime team and the plots in which they find themselves can be even odder. In *The Two-Bear Mambo*, Florida Grange, Leonard's lawyer and Hap's former lover, has disappeared and, when they go in search of her, they find themselves in a town peopled almost exclusively by redneck psychopaths, where voodoo exhumations seem commonplace and the rain pours down in thunderstorms of biblical intensity. In *Bad Chili*, the latest in the series, Leonard becomes the chief suspect in a biker murder, Hap gets bitten by a rabid squirrel and both are the targets of the life-threatening behaviour of the local Chili King. Lansdale's extravagant, profane and bloody narratives are highly recommended.

Bad Chili
Gollancz pbk £9.99 0575065346
Cold in July
Gollancz pbk £5.99 0575400595
Mucho Mojo
Gollancz pbk £5.99 0575400013
Savage Season
Gollancz pbk £5.99 0575400609
The Two-Bear Mambo
Gollancz pbk £5.99 0575400374

Another bad thing about a holding cell is you don't exactly meet a great crowd of people. A lot of them are criminals.'

Joe Lansdale, *Mucho Mojo*

EMMA LATHEN

Martha Henissart and Mary Latsis, writing under the pseudonym of Emma Lathen, have produced a series of well-researched and cleverly characterised crime novels featuring the Wall Street banker/detective John Putnam Thatcher which lift the lid on the murky world of high finance. Only a couple of titles from the series are currently available but these amusing and deftly plotted books are well worth investigating.

East is East
Gollancz pbk £3.99 0575053224

Right on the Money
Gollancz pbk £4.99 057505705X

JANET LAURENCE

For twenty years Janet Laurence has run cookery courses, from basic cookery techniques to tips for the more advanced, and she now divides her time between writing crime fiction and cookery books. She uses her gastronomic knowledge to good effect in her series of novels featuring Darina Lisle, which are designed to appeal to those who love both the pleasures of the table and the pleasures of a well-constructed mystery.

Death à La Provençale
Headline pbk £5.99 0747250820

Death and the Epicure
Headline pbk £5.99 0747242445

Death at the Table
Headline pbk £4.99 0747246017

A Deepe Coffyn
Headline pbk £4.99 0747237727

Diet for Death
Headline pbk £5.99 0747255237

Hotel Morgue
Headline pbk £4.99 0747237743

Recipe for Death
Headline pbk £4.99 0747239568

A Tasty Way to Die
Headline pbk £4.99 0747237735

DONNA LEON

In Donna Leon's series of Venetian detective stories, the reader's guide through the narrative is the humane and sympathetic Commissario Guido Brunetti of the Venice Questura. However the city itself is as much a character as any of the policemen and villains in the books and its *calles* and *campos* are the backdrops for Brunetti's investigations. Brunetti is himself a Venetian with an insider's knowledge of a city unseen by the tourists and he tries hard to balance a quest for truth with the realities and compromises of Venetian, and Italian, politics. These are personified by Brunetti's superior Patta, a man for whom the only acceptable solution is the one which ensures his political advancement. Donna Leon captures ably the ambiguities of Italian crimefighting, in which a simple mugging can lead to the minefields of international corruption and mafia connections, but the strength of these books lies in the characterisation and her evocation of a Venice seen through native eyes and without the gaudy and tawdry tourist trappings.

Acqua Alta
Pan pbk £5.99 0330346261

The Anonymous Venetian
Pan pbk £5.99 0330344129

Death in a Strange Country
Pan pbk £4.99 0330337718

The Death of Faith
Macmillan hbk £16.99 0333673751

A Venetian Reckoning
Pan pbk £4.99 0330344161

ELMORE LEONARD

Elmore Leonard has been writing tough crime fiction for decades. In the eighties he began to gather the sales he deserves and also the reviews. He was acclaimed as one of the greats of the genre. One of his books, *LaBrava*, won the Edgar Allan Poe Award in 1983. In the nineties he has become almost a living legend. *Get Shorty* was acclaimed as a masterpiece by Martin Amis and John Travolta starred in the film version. His writing is so hip that Tarantino is basing his next movie on a Leonard novel. Many of his books have already been made into films and it is easy to see why. Leonard writes with such verve and exhilaration that translation to celluloid seems inevitable. And his fast, funny stories - filled with low-life, weirdos and bad-assed villains - have the kind of dialogue most scriptwriters would kill to achieve. In all his books his slick pace, talent for expertly drawn action and skill with wisecracking and the vernacular dialogue of petty crooks and cops, mark him out as a master of his art.

La Brava
Penguin pbk £4.99 0140072381

Maximum Bob
Penguin pbk £4.99 0140139575

Pronto
Penguin pbk £4.99 0140175717

Riding the Rap
Penguin pbk £4.99 0140250700

Rum Punch
Penguin pbk £4.99 0140139583

Split Images
Penguin pbk £4.99 0140102140

Stick
Penguin pbk £4.99 0140070834

Swag
Penguin pbk £4.99 0140079157

Touch
Penguin pbk £4.99 0140100172

Bandits
Penguin pbk £4.99 0140099050

Cat Chaser
Penguin pbk £4.99 0140089608

City Primeval
Penguin pbk £4.99 0140102132

Freaky Deaky
Penguin pbk £5.99 0140111093

Get Shorty
Penguin pbk £4.99 0140139567

Glitz
Penguin pbk £4.99 0140079254

Gold Coast
Penguin pbk £4.99 0140102159

Killshot
Penguin pbk £5.99 0140111107

AN INTERVIEW WITH ELMORE LEONARD

Nick Rennison speaks to one of the kings of contemporary crime fiction

Elmore Leonard is one of the undisputed kings of crime writing. In book after book he has created an unforgettable and often very funny portrait of the American underworld - of grifters and gangsters, of hoodlums and small-time criminals, mobsters and racketeers. So it seems odd that I am talking to him about Westerns. Yet here we are, a minute into our telephone conversation, and we're talking horse opera rather than crime fiction. Elmore Leonard, it seems, began his writing career by producing Westerns. 'When I graduated I thought, if I'm going to write, I should go about it professionally and look out a genre which had a good market. One where I could learn how to write and sell at the same time. I was also interested in selling to Hollywood. In the fifties Westerns were really big. I hadn't read that many Westerns but I thought that might be a good market to try. So I began to research the South West in the 1880s, learned all I could. All through the fifties the market for Westerns was tremendous. Then, moving into the sixties, two things happened. The market for Western stories dried up - there was so much competition from TV, more than thirty Western series on prime-time TV. And in 1961 I left my job and went freelance. I was doing all sorts of work to make a living - scripts for educational movies for Encyclopedia Britannica, industrial movies on air pollution, stuff like that. I didn't get back to fiction until 1966 when I sold Hombre to Fox and that bought me time to write. So I thought, let's go with crime and see how that works.'

In Leonard's laconic account he started out on the path that was to lead to Harry Arno and Chili Palmer, to books like Get Shorty and Maximum Bob, almost accidentally. I asked him what he'd thought about crime writing at the time he began to write it himself. 'I never cared for real mysteries. Whodunnit, that never interested me. I always felt that the most interesting part of the book was offstage, the stuff dealing with the murderer and who he is. In those books, it was all pretty much one point of view - the detective's - and I wanted to use as many points of view as I could.' Had he always, I wondered, placed the emphasis on dialogue that is apparent in his finest books. 'That's all important to me. Move the story along as much as possible with dialogue, so it's not me telling the reader about somebody's background but two other characters talking about that person's background. I want to write all the scenes from a point of view so that even the narrative takes on the sound of a particular character. When my character looks out the window to see what the weather's like, it's what he thinks of the weather, not what I think.' He pauses at the other end of the line. 'That way, I don't have to wax poetic about the weather. That doesn't interest me. If I open a novel and it starts with the weather, I want to close it.'

And his greatest dialogue goes to his bad guys. The villains get the best lines. His bad guys seem like more fun to write about. 'Yeah, a good guy, a straight arrow, he's gonna behave himself. A bad guy isn't. He's got a negative attitude and that can be funny. My bad guys, though, I try and think of the human side of them. They want pretty much the same thing anybody wants. They want to be happy. They want money. They'll just go about getting it in a different way. They're lazy and they'll cut corners.'

Brilliant though Leonard's characterisation is, he's never developed a series character. One or two of his characters have recurred in later books but he's never created a hero to carry a sequence of books. 'Back in 81 I was going to do it. I had a character in City Primeval, a homicide detective called Raymond Cruz, and my publisher said, 'Put him in the next book and we'll try a continuing character. Maybe that's the way to sell your books. 'So I did and I sent the manuscript of the next book to my agent and he said, 'You've got to change the name of this guy. United Artists owns this character.' They'd bought City Primeval. So I went through the whole manuscript, changed the name all the way through but I missed one place and Raymond still pops up on page 72. People write to me to ask who Raymond is. I leave it there to see if the reader's paying attention.' He's clearly pleased to have created this little test of the reader's concentration but equally clearly doesn't regret the absence of a continuing character. 'I would get bored with that same point of view, novel after novel. John D. McDonald, just before he died, he was on his twenty eighth Travis McGhee book, something like that. He said, 'I don't know if I can deal with this.' He was tired of that guy.'Elmore Leonard may not have created a series character but he has been a prolific and diverse author. Currently he's working on two very different books. 'I'm just beginning a new book with Chili Palmer'. This is the amiable, movie-obsessed mobster from Get Shorty, memorably played by John Travolta in the film of the book, who travels to Hollywood to enforce a debt and ends up as a producer himself. 'This is Chili in the music business. He finds himself even more at home there than he did in the movie business. The kind of characters in the music business are the kind Chili feels comfortable with - not necessarily organised crime people but people who are right next to them.' He's also written a book called Cuba Libre which is a new departure for him. It's set in Cuba one hundred years ago. 'I've always been fascinated by the Spanish-American War of 1898. It was called 'the splendid little war'. There were not many casualties, only about 1500. More were struck down by the yellow fever after the war. The more I researched it, the more I thought that what was interesting was the period just before the war. The Cuban insurgents against the Spanish and some Americans who got involved. So I have this character who arrives three days after the battleship Maine blows up in Havana harbour. He arrives with a string of horses he wants to sell to an American sugar planter and we go from there. And he's got some guns he wants to sell to the insurgents.' We're back with guns and horses, essential ingredients of the Westerns Elmore Leonard began by writing. However he's come a long way from the time when he was selling Western stories to magazines. This is a writer who has, over the last thirty years, created the sharpest and funniest body of work in American crime fiction. Just as well he moved on from guns and horses, if only to return to them eventually.

TED LEWIS

Arguably the finest hardboiled British crime writer ever, Lewis died tragically young after an impressive career as a writer and animator. He is remembered chiefly for the classic novel *Jack's Return Home*, brilliantly filmed as *Get Carter*, with Michael Caine in one of his best roles. Jack Carter is a hardman for hire who works for a London 'firm' run by twin brother gangsters. When his brother dies in suspicious circumstances, Carter's cool and amoral persona is shaken and he travels north to investigate the death. His investigation, accompanied by the icy violence with which he earned his hardman reputation, ruffles the feathers of mobsters both in the north and back in the capital. The skill with which Lewis dovetails his plot makes this a landmark novel and its sequels, although lesser books, are excellent entertainment. Lewis is one of the few British writers to achieve in his books the kind of sparse existentialism achieved by the great American creators of violent and amoral anti-heroes. Jack Carter and the protagonist of Lewis's gangland classic *GBH* are authentic outsiders and the books memorably evoke the shadowy world of pool halls and gambling dens on the borderland between crime and respectability.

Billy Rags
Allison & Busby pbk £6.99
0749001828

GBH
Allison & Busby pbk £4.99
0749001178

Get Carter (Jack's Return Home)
Allison & Busby pbk £3.99
0749001216

Jack Carter's Law
Allison & Busby pbk £4.99
0749001224

Jack Carter & the Mafia Pigeon
Allison & Busby pbk £4.99
0749001771

PETER LOVESEY

One of the most versatile of British crime writers, Lovesey first came to prominence with his series featuring the Victorian police sergeant Cribb and his assistant Constable Thackery. These carefully researched excursions along the byways of nineteenth century society were well received but, sadly, are now out of print. Lovesey's recent novels have included several which involve Bertie, Prince of Wales (later Edward VII) in the unravelling of mysteries and a series of contemporary novels in which the burly detective Peter Diamond, head of the murder squad in Bath, investigates mayhem and misdeeds in the spa town.

Bertie and the Crime of Passion
Warner pbk £4.99 0751509434

Bloodhounds
Warner pbk £5.99 0751518514

Diamond Solitaire
Warner pbk £4.99 0751501603

The Summons
Warner pbk £5.99 0751516279

MARIE BELLOC LOWNDES

(1868–1947)
The sister of the novelist, poet and Catholic polemicist Hilaire Belloc, Marie Belloc Lowndes was a prolific author of stories of crime and mystery, many of them based on real cases. Her only novel to remain in print is *The Lodger*, first published just before the First World War, which describes how a landlady comes to the slow realisation that her apparently genteel lodger is Jack the Ripper. Filmed several times, including once by Alfred Hitchcock, the book retains its interest for both the student of crime fiction and the general reader.

The Lodger
Oxford UP pbk £4.99 019282371X

ARTHUR LYONS

Born in LA in 1946, Arthur Lyons writes straight out of the
hard-boiled tradition of Hammett and Chandler. He also owns
two restaurants in Palm Springs which may account for the critical attention his private eye hero Jacob Asch pays to his food.
Asch is a smooth, wise-cracking detective, streetwise and cynical,
yet showing the same attachment to a personal moral code that
has landed so many fictional detectives, from Spade and
Marlowe onwards, in so much trouble. An ex-journalist who
resigned his job on a matter of principle, Asch is a worthy suc-
cessor to Hammett's and Chandler's heroes. Asch's mean
streets are those trodden by many others in the pulp tradition
but with a contemporary setting. His home territory is Los
Angeles, specifically Hollywood, but the glamour of the film
and TV world serves only as a contrasting backdrop to Asch's
seedy, sleazy surrounds. In the Jacob Asch novels Lyons has created a world of hysterical movie-stars, two-bit junkies, petty
thieves, pimps, prostitutes and corrupt, murderous cops
through which his intelligent and unillusioned hero navigates a
difficult path.

Other People's Money
No Exit Press pbk £4.99 0948353961

ED MCBAIN

Ed McBain is one of the few writers who can be said to have created a sub-genre of fiction single-handedly. Even such originals as Chandler, Hammett and Ross Macdonald had roots in other writers and traditions. The police procedural novel, as written by McBain since the mid-fifties, is, in effect, his own invention. McBain was born Salvatore Lombino in 1926 and changed his name in 1953 to Evan Hunter. Under this name he has published a number of works of mainstream fiction including *The Blackboard Jungle*. However it is under the pseudonym of Ed McBain that he has written his crime fiction and has won his widest readership. Although he has written other crime novels, including twelve featuring Matthew Hope, the 87th Precinct books, of which there are nearly fifty titles, are his best-known work. Steve Carella is the most prominent figure in the stories but the strength of the 87th Precinct books is the ensemble of characters which McBain has created. The professional and personal lives of Carella and his deaf-mute wife Teddy, of Bert Kling, Meyer Meyer, Cotton Hawes and many others are realised and elaborated upon in novels published over several decades. If this formula sounds familiar it is because much of modern American TV crime fiction – *Hill Street Blues* and *NYPD Blue*, for example – derives from it. Perhaps less popular than he once was, McBain remains one of the most prolific and influential of American crime writers.

Beauty and the Beast
Hodder pbk £5.99 0340602961

The Empty Hours
Pan pbk £3.99 0330262793

Ghosts
Hodder pbk £5.99 0340593342

Gladly the Cross-Eyed Bear
Hodder pbk £5.99 0340639873

Goldilocks
Hodder pbk £5.99 0340602988

Guns
Mandarin pbk £3.99 0749309261

Hail, Hail, the Gang's All Here
Hodder pbk £5.99 034059330X

He Who Hesitates
Hodder pbk £5.99 0340593318

The Heckler
Penguin pbk £4.99 0140023933

The House That Jack Built
Warner pbk £5.99 0751513059

Jigsaw
Hodder pbk £5.99 0340593385

Killer's Payoff
Penguin pbk £4.99 0140021191

Lady Killer
Penguin pbk £4.99 0140020195

Long Time No See
Hodder pbk £5.99 0340593326

Lullaby
Pan pbk £4.99 033030822X

Mischief
Hodder pbk £5.99 0340603011

Nocturne
Hodder hbk £16.99 0340695390

Romance
Hodder pbk £5.99 0340638168

Rumpelstiltskin
Hodder pbk £5.99 0340603003

See Them Die
Hodder pbk £5.99 0340593377

Shotgun
Hodder pbk £5.99 0340593393

Ten Plus One
Hodder pbk £5.99 0340593369

There Was a Little Girl
Hodder pbk £5.99 0340639644

Where There's Smoke
Mandarin pbk £3.99 0749309091

HORACE MCCOY

Best remembered as the author of the classic novella *They Shoot Horses, Don't They* (filmed in the Seventies with Jane Fonda and Bruce Dern) McCoy was a gifted writer who produced a number of excellent novels in the Thirties and Forties, as well as short stories for *Black Mask* magazine and numerous screenplays. Although often compared to James M. Cain (at one time McCoy, weary of the comparison, complained to his publishers, 'Continued labelling of me as of 'the Cain school' – whatever the hell that is – and I shall either slit his throat or mine.'), McCoy is closer in style to Jim Thompson, that other hardboiled bard. Like Thompson and many other of the 'tough-guy' writers of the Depression years, McCoy has a strong social element in his work. People are driven to commit crimes not out of venality or lust for power but because they have no direction, no money, no will-power and, most crucially, no choice in the matter. Malign fate plays a significant role in McCoy's work and it is grimly fascinating to watch his characters drift helplessly along, caught in the pull of their inevitable destiny, like scraps of refuse circling nearer to the plug-hole before oblivion beckons. Bleak and nihilistic it may be but, at its best, McCoy's prose has a special kind of resonance that makes it powerful and compelling.

I Should Have Stayed at Home
Serpent's Tail pbk £6.99 1852424028

Kiss Tomorrow Goodbye
Serpent's Tail pbk £6.99 1852424338

They Shoot Horses, Don't They
Serpent's Tail pbk £6.99 185242401X

SHARYN MCCRUMB

Sharyn McCrumb has written more than a dozen novels which have won many awards including an Edgar from the Mystery Writers of America. She is best known, certainly in this country, for the books in what she calls her Ballad series. Set in the hills and hollows of East Tennessee, these tell haunting stories of crimes and misdemeanours, which reflect both the present day dramas of small town life and the long, hard history of the struggle to establish roots and traditions.

The Hangman's Beautiful Daughter
Hodder pbk £5.99 0340646888

If Ever I Return
Hodder pbk £5.99 0340646918

The Rosewood Casket
Hodder pbk £5.99 034064690X

VAL MCDERMID

Val McDermid grew up in a Scottish mining community and worked as a journalist for fourteen years. In 1991 she left journalism to become a full-time writer and in 1995 won the CWA Gold Dagger Award for Best Crime Novel of the Year with *The Mermaids Singing*, a tightly written psychological thriller which explores the tormented mind of a serial killer. McDermid has written two series of novels. Kate Brannigan arrived in *Dead Beat* (1992). This Manchester-based private detective is a sparky and persistent sleuth who spots every wrong move and every line. The novels are complex and pacey but McDermid keeps tight control of the details. The result is tense and satisfying crime reading. Lindsay Gordon hit the scene in *Report for Murder* (1987), one of the first British lesbian mysteries. Gordon is a journalist and reluctant investigator, a strong character who becomes a crime solver by default as her friends hit troubled times. The style of the novels is headlong and pacey, confusions abound and only one person can make sense of them.

Blue Genes
HarperCollins pbk £5.99
0006498310

Booked for Murder
Women's Press pbk £6.99
0704345013

Clean Break
HarperCollins pbk £4.99
0006497721

Common Murder
Women's Press pbk £5.99
0704342065

Crack Down
HarperCollins pbk £4.99
0006490085

Dead Beat
Vista pbk £4.99 0575600020

Final Edition
Women's Press pbk £5.99
070434274X

Kick Back
Vista pbk £4.99 0575600071

The Mermaids Singing
HarperCollins pbk £5.99
0006493580

Report for Murder
Women's Press pbk £5.99
0704340801

Union Jack
Women's Press pbk £6.99
0704343347

QUEER CRIME
by Val McDermid

The author of the Lindsay Gordon novels on the rise
and rise of the dyke detective.

Time was, you had to be a detective to find a queer in a crime novel. And when you did, chances were that they were a villain or victim. But in the 1970s, feminism raised our consciousness and Gay Liberation jerked open the closet door. And when we'd finished a long day of serious politicking, we all wanted somebody strong and sexy to snuggle down with.

Enter the dyke detective.

Cool and in control, tough but tender, the dyke dick has finally come of age in 1997. Manda Scott's first novel, *Hen's Teeth*, was the only genre novel on the short-list for one of Britain's top literary awards, the £30,000 Orange Prize for Fiction. In the US, Joan Drury's *Silent Words* was short-listed for the Mystery Writers of America Edgar Award for best paperback original. And the world's bestselling, highest earning woman crime writer Patricia Cornwell admitted what the world had long suspected - that she too was a lesbian. In 1997, you don't have to look for the logos of the feminist presses to find a lesbian sleuth.

So who is she, this maverick of the main street? And what kind of crime does she investigate?

Back in the pre-feminist days, when the only body-piercing came from guns and knives, lesbians had to be adept at reading the clues in social situations so they could recognise their own kind. In fiction as in life, the closet clues were there for the reader. Who could have read Joyce Porter's deliciously deviant series of black farces featuring the Honourable Constance Ethel Morrison-Burke and not recognised the archetypal butch-femme couple in the Hon. Con and her loyal sidekick Miss Jones? But the L-word is never spoken here, any more than it is in Josephine Tey's *Miss Pym Disposes,* a classic of seething lesbian passions in a women's PE college.

But as our lives came out of the shadows, we wanted heroines with lives we could aspire towards - out and proud, successful in love and feisty enough to put the hetero world in its place. First out of the starting blocks were, inevitably, the Americans. Barbara Wilson, Mary Wings and Katherine V. Forrest blazed a trail with three very different styles of heroine.

Wilson's Pam Nilsen was introduced in *Murder in the Collective*. Pam was that radical archetype, a staunch left-wing feminist with internationalist politics, at home with the rhetoric of agit-prop but, like all of us, susceptible to a pair of beautiful eyes. Wings's Emma Victor gave us a more anarchic take on the politically correct heroine, with a sexy sleuth who wasn't afraid to don a slinky evening dress and high heels ahead of lesbian chic.

Forrest's Kate Delafield, a Los Angeles homicide cop, was in some respects the most traditional of the three, providing a bridge between the classic police procedural novel and the new feminists. Paradoxically, that made her contribution to the mainstreaming of dyke crime all the greater, because she provided easier transition for straight fans of the genre. However, her earlier novels also bolstered the outside world's view of dykedom as a place where you had to be a leather-jacketed butch or a sweetly clinging femme.

I grew up in a world where there were virtually no lesbian role models. The only available check-list came from *The Well of Loneliness*. I knew I didn't want to wear men's suits and ties, I didn't want to be called Stephen and I definitely didn't want to slash my wrists, so I spent most of my late adolescence unaware that I was a dyke.

So when I created Lindsay Gordon, the first 'out' British lesbian detective, I was determined to provide not only a role model but a fantasy figure. I wanted the women who read about her adventures to aspire to being Lindsay's lover or best friend, or the detective herself. That's why she's never described physically in any of the five novels featuring her uniquely stroppy and pig-headed investigative techniques. I wanted her beauty to be firmly in the mind's eye of the beholder.

But these days there is a lesbian detective to suit every fantasy. Sandra Scoppettone's Lauren Laurano is a thirty-something New York sophisticate with a penchant for hanging out on the Internet and an addiction to chocolate; Manda Scott's Dr Kellen Stewart marries leading edge science with ancient magic and holds the world at arms' length while a disorderly queue of admirers waits patiently for her to get her head on straight; Stella Duffy's Saz Martin is a feisty and flirtatious private eye who oozes sensuality and endures affliction stoically; Joan Drury's Tyler Jones is a campaigning journalist with Mother Earth tendencies who knows it's sensible to be scared sometimes. Me, I'm head over heels in love with Laurie King's Kate Martinelli, a San Francisco cop who defines both tenacity and grace under pressure.

As we have grown more assured in our lives as out-and-proud lesbians, so the dyke detective novel has become more confident. In the early examples feminists were Good, men were Bad. It was as if we were trying to persuade ourselves as much as the straight world that all gays were truly wonderful warm-hearted people who would never bitch about another queer. I can still remember the seismic shock that ran through

The Women's Press when I handed in a manuscript with a lesbian murderer.

Now, thankfully, as the gay community moves to a more mature view of itself, the pressure to gloss over the blemishes has gone and dyke crime fiction has grown to reflect our lives in their variegated entirety. That doesn't mean we've become blanded down into homo versions of dull Home Counties life. Because being gay still means a life tinged with risk, our fictions echo that. And they continue to deal with issue that hold particular resonance for the community we are part of; gay parenting, outing, queer-bashing, HIV.

Recently, a British crime writer was overheard complaining that the genre was taken over by 'upstart dykes'. I couldn't help grinning form ear to ear. Time was, you had to be a detective to find a queer in a crime novel. Now it's hard to avoid them. Life's a bitch, and then you murder one.

A version of this article was first published in Pride *magazine.*

Manda Scott
Hen's Teeth
Women's Press pbk £6.99 0704344963

Joan Drury
Silent Words
Women's Press pbk £6.99 0704345226

Barbara Wilson
The Dog Collar Murders
Virago pbk £5.99 1853810665

Barbara Wilson
Gaudi Afternoon
Virago pbk £5.99 1853812641

Barbara Wilson
Murder in the Collective
Virago pbk £5.99 1853816140

Barbara Wilson
Sisters of the Road
Virago pbk £5.99 1853816132

See also entries on Mary Wings, Sandra Scoppettone, Stella Duffy and Laurie King. The crime novels of Joyce Porter and Katherine V. Forrest are currently out of print in the UK.

JOHN D. MACDONALD (1916-1986)

A prodigious producer of pulp fiction in his day, MacDonald remains famous for two things. Firstly the adrenalin-filled novel *The Executioners*, which has been filmed twice, most recently by Martin Scorsese, as *Cape Fear*, and secondly the vast and ambitious series of Travis McGee novels, twenty of them between 1964 and 1985. Working from his houseboat in Bahia Mar, Florida, McGee is a freelance salvage consultant. However, together with his friend, the squat, hairy, immensely wise economist Meyer, he more often salvages lives, reputations and souls than material goods. The plots of these novels are paradigms of construction and McGee's first person narrative is humorous, philosophical and opinionated. The characters are superb- bruised, fragile victims and amoral monsters alike. Above all it is the scope and range of the series that remains so impressive. In the early books the sixties glow is unmistakeable. Beatnik music and bikini babes proliferate. Two decades later, by the time of *The Lonely Silver Rain*, published a year before MacDonald's death, Miami has become a brash, confusing mess of drugs and gang wars. McGee's friends are ageing or dead and there is a melancholy feeling of a real life drawing to a close. There is a direct line of descent from the gothic grandeur of MacDonald's huge work to the thriving sub-genre of Florida crime fiction of today.

The work of John D. Macdonald is currently out of print in the UK. American editions of his novels may be available on import in some larger Waterstone's branches.

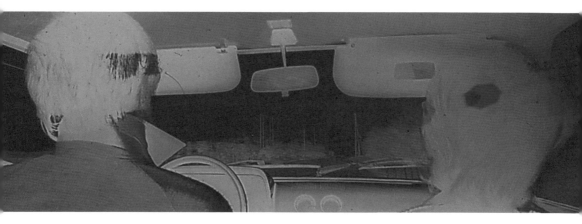

ROSS MACDONALD (1915-1983)

When Ross Macdonald's first book was published in 1944, the Californian private eye novel was in its ascendancy. Raymond Chandler had published his first novel five years earlier and was at the height of his powers, setting the standard which other authors in the field had to match. Ross Macdonald was soon being hailed, by those in the know, as the heir to Chandler's crown. His first few novels seemed to confirm this belief but, as his work progressed, it became very apparent that he was taking his crime stories into territory that no writer then, and few since, have covered. For more than two decades Macdonald (real name Kenneth Millar) wrote intricate and exciting crime novels that reflected the changing nature of Californian society. Lew Archer, Macdonald's private eye, travels through the deserts, forests, canyons, cities and beaches of the West Coast. Embroiled in murder, robbery, extortion and kidnap, he experiences the post-war population boom, the massive expansion of oil-drilling and the destruction of the countryside which were dramatically reshaping the state. Archer, rootless and isolated, was only one of a stream of characters of startling originality in Macdonald's work. The new rich, Mexican immigrants, the decaying old families of California, beach bums, small town police officers, no-hope ex-cons - all play their roles in Archer's investigations. Driven, in different ways, in search of the American dream, they are ruthlessly dissected in Macdonald's fiction. Certainly Macdonald continued the tradition established by Chandler but he shaped and moulded it in ways that were uniquely his own.

Blue City
Allison & Busby pbk £6.99
0749001992

The Instant Enemy
Allison & Busby pbk £6.99
0749002433

Lew Archer Omnibus 1
Allison & Busby pbk £8.99
0749001097

Lew Archer Omnibus 2
Allison & Busby pbk £8.99
0749002018

Lew Archer Omnibus 3
Allison & Busby pbk £9.99
0749003405

Meet Me at the Morgue
Allison & Busby pbk £4.99
0850317118

Sleeping Beauty
Allison & Busby pbk £6.99
0749001623

The Underground Man
Allison & Busby pbk £4.99
0749002069

The Wycherly Woman
Allison & Busby pbk £3.99
0749001054

The Zebra-Striped Hearse
Allison & Busby pbk £3.99
0749001453

'The name is Archer, Lew Archer, private detective in the land of dreams – California; in the land of peaches and honey, misery and murder – male and female!

... if you stick a lighted match into a barrel of gasoline, something's going to happen, and as far as men are concerned that's what women are – a lighted match.'

Ross MacDonald

WILLIAM McILVANNEY

The gifted and acclaimed Scottish novelist and poet has written a number of books in which the protagonists, possesssed of traditional, male working class values, are confronted by circumstances that test those values to the limit. His three novels featuring the maverick Glaswegian police inspector Jack Laidlaw successfully transfer this struggle to the crime fiction genre.

Laidlaw
Hodder pbk £5.99 0340207272

The Papers of Tony Veitch
Hodder pbk £5.99 0340576898

Strange Loyalties
Hodder pbk £5.99 0340574607

JILL McGOWN

Jill McGown published her first novel in 1983 and has since produced a series of titles featuring Detective Inspector Lloyd and Sergeant Judy Hill. These well-constructed and well written mysteries are in the best tradition of the English detective story and yet engagingly and unmistakably contemporary.

The Murders of Mrs Austin and Mrs Beale
Pan pbk £4.99 0330319396

The Other Woman
Pan pbk £4.99 0330329855

A Perfect Match
Pan pbk £4.99 0330315811

A Shred of Evidence
Pan pbk £5.99 0330346172

NGAIO MARSH (1899–1982)

Ngaio Marsh, creator of Inspector Roderick Alleyn, continues to be one of the most widely read authors of the golden age of crime fiction. She was born in New Zealand and began her career as an actress and theatrical producer. Several of her novels are set in her native country and an interest in the arts is a recurring theme in her work. She writes with gusto about actors and artists and books such as *Opening Night, Death at the Dolphin, Enter a Murderer* and *Vintage Murder*, set in and around the theatre, demonstrate a love of theatre mingled with a wry appreciation of the excesses of that world. Other novels exploit equally intriguing settings - from a sheep farm to a satanic ring in rural France - and, like her settings, the murders in her books are always inventive and unexpected. However her greatest success was the creation of Inspector Alleyn, the urbane and sharp-witted detective whose commanding presence holds together the disparate elements of plot and character in her crime fiction.

Artists in Crime
HarperCollins pbk £4.99
000616529X

Black As He's Painted
HarperCollins pbk £4.99
0006138403

Clutch of Constables
HarperCollins pbk £4.99
0006165311

Colour Scheme
HarperCollins pbk £4.99
0006163769

Dead Water
HarperCollins pbk £4.99
000616465X

Death & the Dancing Footman
HarperCollins pbk £4.99
0006169023

Death at the Bar
HarperCollins pbk £4.99
000616532X

Death at the Dolphin
HarperCollins pbk £4.99
0006167918

Death in Ecstasy
HarperCollins pbk £4.99
0006157440

Death on the Air
HarperCollins pbk £4.99
0006477135

Died in the Wool
HarperCollins pbk £4.99
0006161510

Enter a Murderer
HarperCollins pbk £4.99
0006156509

False Scent
HarperCollins pbk £4.99
0006155901

Final Curtain
HarperCollins pbk £4.99
0006159575

Hand in Glove
HarperCollins pbk £4.99
0006166296

Last Ditch
HarperCollins pbk £4.99
0006168949

Light Thickens
HarperCollins pbk £4.99
0006167934

A Man Lay Dead
HarperCollins pbk £4.99
000615591X

The Nursing Home Murder
HarperCollins pbk £4.99
0006123961

Off With His Head
HarperCollins pbk £4.99
0006169198

Opening Night
HarperCollins pbk £4.99
0006157742

Overture to Death
HarperCollins pbk £4.99
0006167594

Photo-Finish
HarperCollins pbk £4.99
0006170714

Scales of Justice
HarperCollins pbk £4.99
0006157777

Singing in the Shrouds
HarperCollins pbk £4.99
0006159583

Spinsters in Jeopardy
HarperCollins pbk £4.99
0006165305

Surfeit of Lampreys
HarperCollins pbk £4.99
000612412X

Swing, Brother, Swing
HarperCollins pbk £4.99
0006164412

Tied Up in Tinsel
HarperCollins pbk £4.99
0006158323

Vintage Murder
HarperCollins pbk £4.99
0006161529

When in Rome
HarperCollins pbk £4.99
0006157459

A. E. MARSTON

For more than thirty years A. E. Marston has worked as a freelance writer, producing novels and children's books as well as plays for radio, television and the theatre. Recently he has drawn on this wealth of experience, and from his previous career as a history lecturer, to write a sequence of well-received historical mysteries set at the time of the Domesday survey. In the books the Domesday commissioners Ralph Delchard and Gervase Bret make their way around the country, intent on settling land and property disputes, but certain to stumble across murder and macabre mysteries that also demand their attention. The series is well-written, filled with historical detail and thoroughly entertaining.

The Dragons of Archenfield
Headline pbk £5.99 0747249482

The Lions of the North
Headline pbk £5.99 074725415X

The Ravens of Blackwater
Headline pbk £5.99 0747248966

The Serpents of Harbledown
Headline pbk £5.99 0747254168

The Wolves of Savernake
Headline pbk £5.99 0747247676

MARGARET MILLAR

It is, perhaps, fitting that Margaret Millar, born in Canada, should work comfortably on the dividing line between the cosy mysteries of the classic English school of detective fiction and their much harder-boiled American counterparts. A large number of her many novels have a strong legal theme and she creates marvellous courtroom scenes in which the reader is often made to feel like a member of the jury, watching breathlessly as the defendant shifts uneasily under questioning or waiting for the dramatic interruption of the judge's gavel. Unlike many crime writers, including her husband Ross MacDonald, Millar avoids using a single detective/narrator to carry her stories but entrusts them to a rich and memorable gallery of characters. For over forty years she produced a consistently entertaining stream of books but the fifties were probably her peak years, culminating in her 1955 novel *Beast in View* which won the Edgar Allan Poe award from the Mystery Writers of America. In addition to this justly celebrated classic *The Soft Talkers, Stranger in My Grave, How Like an Angel* and *Ask for Me Tomorrow* are all highly recommended.

Ask for Me Tomorrow
Allison & Busby pbk £3.99 0749000996

Banshee
Allison & Busby pbk £4.99 0749002751

How Like An Angel
Allison & Busby pbk £6.99 0749002786

Mermaid
Allison & Busby pbk £3.99 0749001100

Rose's Last Summer
Allison & Busby pbk £4.99 0749001968

The Soft Talkers
Allison & Busby pbk £6.99 0749002883

A Stranger in My Grave
Allison & Busby pbk £6.99 0749002239

GLADYS MITCHELL (1901–1983)

'The Great Gladys' is how crime fiction fan Philip Larkin described Gladys Mitchell and for more than fifty years she produced a steady stream of classic detective novels. Very little of what she wrote is currently in print, which is a great pity, since she was one of the most talented of the writers of the golden age of English detective fiction, and Dame Beatrice Lestrange Bradley, psychiatric advisor to the Home Office, who appeared in more than sixty books, is one of the most eccentric and compelling creations in whodunnit literature.

Death at the Opera
Warner pbk £4.99 074740254X

The Rising of the Moon
Virago pbk £5.99 1860490743

A number of other Gladys Mitchell titles are available in hardback library editions and could be ordered through Waterstone's branches.

MANUEL VASQUEZ MONTALBAN

Born and bred in Barcelona, Montalban is the author of five highly acclaimed novels featuring private detective Pepe Carvalho. Carvalho is a splendid creation – a gourmet, quick-witted and a lover of the fast life. As a former member of the Spanish Communist Party and an ex-employee of the CIA, he is ideally equipped to investigate delicate matters such as murder, even though his dionysian appetites are frowned upon by both his erstwhile employees. Montalban's books are almost impossible to fault. They all succeed on a number of levels and each one is like a delicious meal. They contain ingredients of the classic private eye novels. Carvalho, despite the presence of his sidekick Biscuter, is essentially a loner, too much of an individual to fit in with austere, if corrupt, organisations. Furthermore, he's a man who can get the job done but wants to indulge his fondness for food, drink and women along the way. He's a kind of picaresque, Catalan version of Philip Marlowe. As in all the best noir fiction, the city – in this case, Carvalho's beloved Barcelona – is superbly realised and becomes almost a character its own right. Add to all this the social history and political realism in which the books are steeped and the result is the feast for crime fans which Montalban provides.

The Angst-Ridden Executive
Serpent's Tail pbk £7.99 1852421592

Murder in the Central Committee
Serpent's Tail pbk £7.99 1852421312

Off Side
Serpent's Tail pbk £8.99 1852422084

An Olympic Death
Serpent's Tail pbk £7.99 1852422572

SUSAN MOODY

A former chairwoman of the Crime Writers' Association, Susan Moody has been a prolific and highly praised author of suspense and detective fiction for a number of years. Her first series character was Penny Wanawake, the daughter of an African diplomat father and an English aristocratic mother, with a taste for adventure and a cat burglar for a boyfriend. More recently she has published books in another series, the heroine of which is a professional bridge player, Cassie Swann.

Doubled in Spades
Headline pbk £5.99 0747246254

Grand Slam
Headline pbk £4.99 0747239479

King of Hearts
Headline pbk £4.99 0747246246

The Sacrifice Bid
Headline hbk £16.99 0747219060

Takeout Double
Headline pbk £4.99 0747239460

IAN MORSON

The success of Ellis Peters's creation Brother Cadfael has meant that a large number of other medieval detectives have arrived on the scene in the last few years, to meet the public's demand for historical crime fiction. Ian Morson's Regent Master William Falconer, teacher in thirteenth century Oxford and advocate of Aristotelian logic in the investigation of crimes, has appeared in only a handful of novels but has already proved to be one of the more engaging of the recent arrivals.

Falconer and the Face of God
Gollancz pbk £5.99 0575600632

Falconer's Crusade
Gollancz pbk £4.99 0575600799

Falconer's Judgement
Gollancz pbk £4.99 0575600047

A Psalm for Falconer
Gollancz hbk £15.99 0575060468

WALTER MOSLEY

Born in Los Angeles to a black Louisianan father and a white Jewish mother, Mosley studied political science at Johnson State College and at the University of Massachusetts before working as a computer programmer in New York. Encouraged by his wife and friends, he enrolled in 1985 on a graduate writing programme at the City College of New York. His first novel was *Gone Fishin'* which introduced the characters of Ezekiel 'Easy' Rawlins and his dangerously volatile friend Raymond 'Mouse' Alexander. This was turned down repeatedly by publishers and was finally published in 1997 after later novels had brought him success and, famously, his status as Bill Clinton's favourite novelist. Beginning with *Devil in a Blue Dress*, Mosley has created what is, simultaneously, a series of first-class crime novels and a telling but unpretentious account of the black experience in America from the 1940s to the 1960s. Rawlins, transformed from the teenager of *Gone Fishin'*, is a tough war veteran who takes up detective work in Los Angeles and is drawn into the hotbed of racial tensions and political and moral ambiguities that informs life in the city. Mosley is a skilful storyteller and his control over plot, dialogue and characters is exemplary. Not a word is wasted in these taut and realistic stories. His latest book, *Always Outnumbered, Always Outgunned*, is a series of short stories featuring a new character, Socrates Fortlow.

Always Outnumbered, Always Outgunned
Serpent's Tail hbk £11.99 1852425180

Black Betty
Pan pbk £4.99 0330334719

Devil in a Blue Dress
Pan pbk £4.99 0330321145

Gone Fishin'
Serpent's Tail hbk £9.99 1852425792

A Little Yellow Dog
Pan pbk £6.99 0330334727

A Red Death
Pan pbk £4.99 0330321153

Walter Mosley Omnibus
Picador pbk £8.99 0330336266

White Butterfly
Pan pbk £4.99 0330330535

MARCIA MULLER

In 1977 Marcia Muller published the first of her Sharon McCone novels, *Edwin of the Iron Shoes*, and thus earned her reputation as the founding mother of the contemporary female private eye novel. In the ensuing two decades Muller has written a series of books in which the plots have become increasingly elaborate and the character of McCone - independent, sensitive yet tough, occasionally irrational - increasingly complex and believable. The McCone novels are excellent examples of mysteries in which plot and storyline emerge naturally from character and from sense of place. (McCone works primarily in San Francisco and Muller captures well that city's vibrancy.) McCone has been embroiled in the dangerous worlds of terrorism, international art fraud and, in one of her recent novels *The Broken Promise Land*, the murky waters of the music industry. In each novel Marcia Muller has demonstrated that she is not only a pioneer in a crime sub-genre, one who has had many imitators, but that she remains one of its ablest exponents.

Ask the Cards a Question
Women's Press pbk £5.99
0704343657

Both Ends of the Night
Women's Press pbk £5.99
070434551X

The Broken Promise Land
Women's Press pbk £6.99
0704345048

Edwin of the Iron Shoes
Women's Press pbk £5.99
0704343649

Games to Keep the Dark Away
Women's Press pbk £5.99
0704343681

Leave a Message for Willie
Women's Press pbk £5.99
070434369X

Pennies on a Dead Woman's Eyes
Women's Press pbk £5.99
0704343371

The Shape of Dread
Women's Press pbk £5.99
0704343134

There's Something in a Sunday
Women's Press pbk £5.99
0704343126

Till the Butchers Cut Him Down
Women's Press pbk £5.99
0704344165

Trophies and Dead Things
Women's Press pbk £5.99
0704343142

Where Echoes Live
Women's Press pbk £5.99
0704343150

A Wild and Lonely Place
Women's Press pbk £5.99
0704344548

Wolf in the Shadows
Women's Press pbk £5.99
0704343894

AMY MYERS

Amy Myers has worked in publishing and as a freelance editor and writer. Her series of Victorian whodunnits, featuring the chef and mystery solver Auguste Didier, are entertainingly written and crammed with enjoyable period detail. She has also written mysteries under the pseudonym of Laura Daniels.

Murder at Plum's
Headline pbk £4.50 0747233977

Murder at the Masque
Headline pbk £3.99 0747236747

Murder at the Music Hall
Headline pbk £5.99 0747248435

Murder in the Limelight
Headline pbk £4.99 0747231788

Murder in the Motor Stable
Headline pbk £5.99 0747248443

Murder in the Smokehouse
Headline pbk £4.99 074724328X

Murder Makes an Entree
Headline pbk £4.50 0747238480

Murder Under the Kissing Bough
Headline pbk £4.99 0747240140

AS LAURA DANIELS

The Lakenham Folly
Headline pbk £5.99 074724927X

Pleasant Vices
Headline pbk £5.99 0747246831

MAGDALEN NABB

Magdalen Nabb has lived in Florence for more than twenty years and pursues a dual career as crime writer and children's author. Her series of novels about Marshal Guarnaccia of the carabinieri has been highly acclaimed both for its evocation of the dark side of Florence, the side the tourists don't see, and for its psychological acuity.

The Marshal at the Villa Torini
HarperCollins pbk £4.99
0006478913

The Marshal Makes His Report
HarperCollins pbk £4.99
0006496954

The Monster of Florence
HarperCollins pbk £5.99
0006499511

REGGIE NADELSON

Reggie Nadelson has so far published two of her riveting mysteries featuring Artie Cohen, ex-special detective with the New York police department. In *Red Mercury Blues* the killing on live TV of a former KGB general marks the beginning of a complicated plot in which the vital ingredient, sought by all, is 'red mercury', an essential component in the making of nuclear weapons. In *Hot Poppies* a murder in New York's diamond department sets Cohen on a trail which leads him from the Big Apple to London's Chinatown to Hong Kong in pursuit of a deadly trade in human beings.

Hot Poppies
Faber hbk £14.99 0571174353
Red Mercury Blues
Faber pbk £5.99 0571173853

JANET NEEL

Bloody boardroom coups and treacherous takeovers are regular occurrences in the financial world. Corruption may flourish but literal murder is less frequent. The two forces that investigate these crimes combine in Janet Neel's elegant mystery series set in the City of London. Her two protagonists, Francesca Wilson of the DTI and Detective Inspector John McLeish of the CID, meet and clash when her financial investigations overlap with his murder inquiries. The interplay betwen these two appealing characters – a strong and intelligent woman and a humorous, self-deprecating man – is one of the strengths of the series. Neel, a solicitor and an administrator in the Department of Trade and Industry, writes with an insider's authority of the intricate machinations in the City, where transactions of billions of pounds are commonplace and where, at least in the novels, the unspoken assumptions of power and money make financiers forget the commandment – 'Thou Shalt Not Kill'. She has won several awards for her writing. *Death's Bright Angel* won the 1988 John Creasey Award for best first crime novel and *Death of a Partner* and *Death Among the Dons* were shortlisted for the CWA Gold Dagger Award. She has also written non-genre fiction under her real name of Janet Cohen.

Death Among the Dons
Penguin pbk £4.99 0140230572
Death of A Partner
Penguin pbk £4.99 0140145877
Death on Site
Penguin pbk £4.99 0140129944
Death's Bright Angel
Penguin pbk £5.99 0140114955
A Timely Death
Penguin pbk £5.99 0140259678

INGRID NOLL

Ingrid Noll was born in Shanghai to German parents in 1935. In Germany her crime novels are massive bestsellers and, inevitably but unimaginatively, newspapers in this country have dubbed her 'Germany's Queen of Crime'. Potential readers should not be deterred by this less than enticing soubriquet. Writing darkly comic, psychological thrillers in the manner of Patricia Highsmith or Barbara Vine, she is an original and highly gifted writer whose works may yet become the bestsellers in Britain that they are in Europe.

Head Count
HarperCollins pbk £8.99
000232640X
Hell Hath No Fury
HarperCollins pbk £5.99
0006497667

CAROL O'CONNELL

Carol O'Connell is a major new talent in crime writing and her first few novels have achieved both commercial and critical success. Much of this is due to the startling originality of her police detective heroine Kathy Mallory, whose bizarre and enigmatic personality dominates the books. Maverick cops are ten a penny in crime fiction but Mallory - she prefers not to use her first name, seeing it as too personal - is a genuinely unsettling and unforgettable creation. The adoptive daughter of a legendary New York cop she has been at home in the world of homicide investigation since her early teens. Exceptionally intelligent, she is also unnaturally self-contained and dedicated to the job, unforgiving of herself and others. Her will to unearth the truths that others would prefer to keep hidden, while maintaining her own inscrutability, is what drives the tension in these witty and memorable thrillers.

Flight of the Stone Angel
Hutchinson hbk £10.00 0091801559
Killing Critics
Arrow pbk £5.99 0099163926
Mallory's Oracle
Arrow pbk £4.99 0099433818
The Man Who Lied to Women
Arrow pbk £4.99 0099433710

SARA PARETSKY

Kansas-born Paretsky remains one of the leading American crime writers and Vic Warshawski, her chic Chicago private eye, remains the model for many feisty female detectives in contemporary fiction. She is tough, stubborn and emotional. She likes her whisky. She is not shy of becoming personally involved with the cases she takes on and she shows more tenacity than most when the going gets rough. She has a capacity for taking the sort of physical and psychological punishment that would floor a lesser woman. What raises Warshawski well beyond cliche, however, is Paretsky's eye for everyday details - the details of how Warshawski dresses, what she eats, of the Chicago streets on which she operates. Warshawski becomes a thinking, feeling, totally believable heroine and Paretsky's well-written dialogue and adroit plotting add to the quality of the books in which she appears.

Bitter Medicine
Penguin pbk £5.99 0140113053
Burn Marks
Virago pbk £6.99 185381279X
Deadlock
Penguin pbk £5.99 014009255
Guardian Angel
Penguin pbk £5.99 0140170677
Indemnity Order
Penguin pbk £5.99 0140099247
Killing Orders
Penguin pbk £5.99 0140099263
Toxic Shock
Penguin pbk £5.99 0140124098
Tunnel Vision
Penguin pbk £5.99 0140170812
V. I. for Short
Penguin pbk £5.99 0140251235
V. I. Warshawski Omnibus
Penguin pbk £9.99 014023151X

ROBERT B. PARKER

Since being called in to locate a missing 14th century manuscript in *The Godwulf Manuscript* in 1974, Robert B. Parker's private detective hero Spenser has appeared in over twenty books which rank amongst the most reliable and satisfying of American P.I. novels. Through the series the regular cast of characters has remained remarkably consistent – policemen working in the 70s are still clocking on in the 90s and Susan, Spenser's psychologist lover, first appears as a school counsellor in *God Save the Child* in 1974. Parker's style is anything but flashy but the sense of place and period always rings true. Spenser's cases are based mainly in and around Boston which allows for a variety of settings from Chinatowns and black ghettoes to WASP enclaves and universities. Parker himself has been a professor of literature and has written a book on weight training, and his alter ego, Spenser, is a man of intellectual and physical strength. He is literate and witty, sensitive to political issues of gender and race (his long-term sexual partner is Jewish, his detecting partner black) and able to discuss his cases with Susan in terms of their psychological and sociological contexts. But he is also decidedly heterosexual, capable of extreme violence and quite at ease in the company of career criminals. Parker writes very much within the tradition exemplified by Raymond Chandler and he was chosen to complete Chandler's *Poodle Springs*, published in 1989. In many ways Spenser is Marlowe's direct descendant. The streets may be a little less mean, the wit a little less biting and the politics a little more correct but the writing is so assured and the story-telling so satisfying that Spenser's longevity is guaranteed.

All Our Yesterdays
Penguin pbk £5.99 0140239960

A Catskill Eagle
Penguin pbk £5.99 0140084754

Ceremony
Penguin pbk £4.99 0140089535

Crimson Joy
Penguin pbk £5.99 0140116508

Double Deuce
Penguin pbk £5.99 0140171339

God Save the Child
Penguin pbk £4.99 014004471X

The Godwulf Manuscript
Penguin pbk £4.99 014004132X

Pale Kings and Princes
Penguin pbk £5.99 0140105891

Playmates
Penguin pbk £5.99 014012652X

Thin Air
Penguin pbk £5.99 014025207X

Walking Shadow
Penguin pbk £5.99 0140175563

The Widening Gyre
Penguin pbk £5.99 0140089551

Wilderness
Penguin pbk £5.99 0140055592

JAMES PATTERSON

James Patterson, author of a series of 'nursery rhyme' mysteries, looks set to be the next major star of crime fiction. The first in the series, *Along Came a Spider*, introduced the reader to Alex Cross, a black detective with a Ph.D in psychology and a pair of rock-hard fists, and was a bestseller. So, too, was *Kiss the Girls* which also featured Cross and was made into a film starring Morgan Freeman in the central role. Cross does not appear in Patterson's third novel, *Hide and Seek*, which is narrated by its two principal characters in alternating chapters, an old trick but one which Patterson pulls off quite well. However he re-appeared in *Jack and Jill* and also features in *Cat and Mouse*, Patterson's latest offering, which may well be the book to catapult him from the ranks of the merely bestselling into superstardom as an author.

Along Came a Spider
HarperCollins pbk £5.99
0006476155

Black Market
HarperCollins pbk £5.99
0006493149

Cat and Mouse
Headline hbk £16.99 0747220220

Hide and Seek
HarperCollins pbk £5.99
0006498523

Jack and Jill
HarperCollins pbk £6.99
0006493122

Kiss the Girls
HarperCollins pbk £6.99
0006499724

MICHAEL PEARCE

Pearce grew up in what was then the Anglo-Egyptian Sudan and has spent part of his career teaching there, and he draws upon his knowledge of that part of the world and its history in his unusual series of detective novels. His central character is Gareth Owen, otherwise known as the Mamur Zapt and the head of Cairo's secret police in the years before the First World War, who operates amid the swirling religious and political tensions of an Egypt under imperial rule. Pearce devises his plots with intricate skill and relates them with a wry, tongue-in-cheek humour that makes the Mamur Zapt series a delight to read.

The Camel of Destruction
HarperCollins pbk £4.99 0006478921

The Mamur Zapt and the Donkey-Vous
HarperCollins pbk £3.50 0006471080

The Mamur Zapt and the Men Behind
HarperCollins pbk £4.99 0006472664

The Mamur Zapt and the Night of the Dog
HarperCollins pbk £3.50 0006471099

The Mingrelian Conspiracy
HarperCollins pbk £4.99 0006497780

The Snake-Catcher's Daughter
HarperCollins pbk £4.99 0006490360

IAIN PEARS

Art historian and author of the much-praised historical novel *An Instance of the Fingerpost*, Pears is also the writer of an engaging series of crime novels set in the Italian art-world. His hero, the English art dealer Jonathan Argyll, works in tandem with Italy's Art Theft Squad to unmask fraudulence, larceny and murder. In *Death and Restoration*, the most recent in the series, Argyll, together with his girlfriend Flavia di Stefano immerse themselves in the intrigues of monastic and police politics as they investigate the seemingly senseless theft of an unremarkable icon from the monastery of San Giovanni and its connection with a body found in the Tiber. Pears's deft combination of expert knowledge with dry, ironic humour gives the series a particular charm.

Death and Restoration
HarperCollins pbk £5.99
0006498752

Giotto's Hand
HarperCollins pbk £4.99
0006490263

GEORGE PELECANOS

In Nick Stefanos - music fan, ardent drinker and reluctant private eye - Pelecanos has created an instant hard-boiled classic. Effortlessly he's taken the mould of Philip Marlowe, dropped it in a double bourbon and served up a masterful cocktail. Like all noir heroes, Nick is a man running from his past and taking most of it with him. Alcohol and guilt (in equally large measures) provide the fuel that keeps him running; murder is usually the obstacle that stops him in his tracks. So far Pelecanos has given us two Stefanos novels. *Firing Offense*, the first (although the latest to be published in this country), is an excellent debut as Nick searches for a young work colleague, is fired from his job, discovers his ex-employers are running a drug-smuggling ring and encounters much bloodshed and violence. *Down by the River Where the Dead Men Go*, the second novel, sees Nick, now bartending, still battling his demons between bouts of binge drinking. He's also hot on the trail of some pornographers in the hunt for a murderer. Violence erupts, drenching the pages with spilled blood and booze. Eventually Nick wraps up the case with a final yet redemptive act of violence, leaving readers thirsting for more Stefanos novels.

Down by the River Where the Dead Men Go
Serpent's Tail pbk £8.99 1852425296

A Firing Offense
Serpent's Tail pbk £8.99 1852425636

DANIEL PENNAC

Recent French detective fiction has been dominated by the
Benjamin Malaussene quartet of novels by Daniel Pennac.
Pennac takes the surreal and streetwise elements of Delacorta's
thrillers of the eighties and combines them with anarchic
incident and a gallery of extraordinary characters, to produce
immensely entertaining stories that are vividly contemporary. In
the first novel to be published in English, *The Fairy Gunmother*,
we meet Malaussene, a professional scapegoat whose talent for
disarming people is invaluable in deflecting complaints to
department stores and publishers. His domestic life is a web of
Byzantine complexity including numerous heroin-addicted
grandfathers, siblings of varying degrees of sanity and an
epileptic dog. Events bring them all into contact with the local
police force, comprised of transvestites, racists and saintly
interrogators. Meanwhile somebody is cutting the wrinkled
throats of old ladies . . . Pennac's effortlessly floating narrative
voice and liberal use of Parisian street slang brilliantly evoke the
vitality of the seething, multi-racial Belleville quartier and the
translation by Ian Monk is masterful. Harvill plan to publish the
remaining three novels in the near future.

The Fairy Gunmother
Harvill pbk £9.99 1860463266

ANNE PERRY

Since she published her first novel in 1978, Anne Perry has been a prolific writer of murder mysteries set in Victorian London. Her work has long been popular in the States and now her two series of books, one featuring the husband and wife team of Thomas and Charlotte Pitt, and the other the saturnine police detective William Monk, are enjoying a growing reputation in this country for their historical detail and convincing characterisation.

Belgrave Square
HarperCollins pbk £4.99
0006479073

Bluegate Fields
HarperCollins pbk £4.99
0006479057

Cain His Brother
Headline pbk £5.99 0747248451

A Dangerous Mourning
Headline pbk £5.99 0747245266

Defend and Betray
Headline pbk £5.99 0747248702

The Face of A Stranger
Headline pbk £5.99 0747243557

Farriers' Lane
HarperCollins pbk £4.99
0006479138

Highgate Rise
HarperCollins pbk £4.99
0006479065

The Hyde Park Headsman
HarperCollins pbk £5.99
0006479146

A Silent Cry
Headline hbk £16.99 074725253X

Sins of the Wolf
Headline pbk £5.99 0747246327

A Sudden Fearful Death
Headline pbk £5.99 0747242887

Weighed in the Balance
Headline pbk £5.99 0747252521

CHARLES PERRY (1924–1969)

Perry was a black radio actor and playwright who published *Portrait of a Young Man Drowning*, his only novel, in America in 1962. This extraordinary and unique book begins as a pastiche of Joyce's *Portrait of the Artist as a Young Man* but rapidly gains its own momentum as it tells the story of Harold, a young man sucked into the underworld of Brooklyn. As Harold progresses further up the gangster echelons he becomes increasingly paranoid and out of control, driven inexorably towards madness and murder. This is the first British publication of a cult novel. Perry himself was working on a semi-autobiographical account of the murder of his eleven year old son, entitled *I Wake Up Screaming*, when he was diagnosed with terminal cancer. The manuscript was lost after his death.

Portrait of a Young Man Drowning
Payback Press pbk £6.99 0862416027

ELLIS PETERS

Although Ellis Peters wrote many crime novels and historical novels both under that name and under her real name Edith Pargeter, it is for her Chronicles of Brother Cadfael that she is most loved and remembered. The chronicles start in 1137 with *A Morbid Taste of Bones* and finish in 1145 with *Brother Cadfael's Penance*. They follow the exploits of Brother Cadfael, a highly unusual Welsh monk and herbalist, who came late to his calling by way of the Crusades and ten years as a sea captain against the corsairs. He is to be found most often in his workshop and herb garden at the Benedictine Abbey of Saint Peter and Saint Paul in Shrewsbury, although, in several of the books, he takes authorised and unauthorised excursions elsewhere if his services are needed. The historical setting for the series is the long and arduous civil war between King Stephen and the Empress Maud which caused suffering and hardship throughout England. The man charged with keeping the peace in Shrewsbury and the surrounding country is Hugh Beringar who first appears in *One Corpse Too Many* when he is appointed deputy sheriff of Shropshire. In later books he rises to sheriff. The friendship between Cadfael and Beringar progresses through the chronicles, as do their skills as detectives. While Beringar follows the usual paths of law enforcement for the period, Brother Cadfael uses forensic clues to help solve the wrongdoings which occur in and around the precincts of the Abbey. It is Cadfael who has the ability to ask the most pertinent questions about the crimes. Why would a corpse have a certain weed which only grows in one place about his person? Why does a wound supposedly made by a sword have all the characteristics of a dagger wound? This ability and his powers of deduction lead him to the true wrongdoer in each case. Throughout all the twenty novels historical fact is blended smoothly with fiction as the reader is taken season by season through the lives of the monks and people of medieval Shropshire and the Marches. Ellis Peters' skills as a deviser of medieval mysteries have made Cadfael a popular character in detective fiction for some years and that popularity has recently been enhanced by the TV series starring Derk Jacobi.

BROTHER CADFAEL SERIES

A Morbid Taste for Bones
Warner pbk £5.99 0751517496

One Corpse Too Many
Warner pbk £5.99 0751511021

Monk's-Hood
Warner pbk £5.99 075151103X

St. Peter's Fair
Warner pbk £5.99 0751514004

The Leper of Saint Giles
Warner pbk £5.99 0751511056

The Virgin in the Ice
Warner pbk £5.99 0751514012

The Sanctuary Sparrow
Warner pbk £5.99 0751511072

The Devil's Novice
Warner pbk £5.99 0751513997

Dead Man's Ransom
Warner pbk £5.99 0751511099

The Pilgrim of Hate
Warner pbk £4.99 0751511102

An Excellent Mystery
Warner pbk £5.99 0751511110

A Rare Benedictine
Headline pbk £5.99 0747234205

The Raven in the Foregate
Warner pbk £5.99 0751517402

The Rose Rent
Warner pbk £5.99 0751517410

The Hermit of Eyton Forest
Warner pbk £5.99 0751502243

The Confession of Brother Haluin
Warner pbk £5.99 0751511153

The Heretic's Apprentice
Warner pbk £5.99 0751511161

The Potter's Field
Warner pbk £5.99 075151117X

The Summer of the Danes
Warner pbk £5.99 0751511188

The Holy Thief
Warner pbk £5.99 0751511196

Brother Cadfael's Penance
Warner pbk £5.99 0751513709

The Cadfael Omnibus
Warner pbk £10.99 0751504769

The Second Cadfael Omnibus
Warner pbk £10.99 0751507296

The Third Cadfael Omnibus
Warner pbk £10.99 0751501115

The Fourth Cadfael Omnibus
Warner pbk £10.99 0751503924

The Fifth Cadfael Omnibus
Warner pbk £10.99 0751509493

The Sixth Cadfael Omnibus
Warner pbk £10.99 0751515892

The Seventh Cadfael Omnibus
Warner pbk £10.99 0751520810

Ellis Peters was also the author of a series of contemporary crime stories featuring Inspector George Felse.

GEORGE FELSE SERIES

Black Is the Colour of My True Love's Heart
Warner pbk £4.99 0751512338

Death and the Joyful Woman
Warner pbk £3.99 0708849539

Fallen into the Pit
Warner pbk £4.99 0751512230

The Grass Widow's Tale
Warner pbk £3.99 0708849954

The House of Green Turf
Warner pbk £4.50 0708854257

The Knocker on Death's Door
Warner pbk £3.99 0708842410

A Nice Derangement of Epitaphs
Warner pbk £4.50 0708837514

Rainbow's End
Warner pbk £4.99 0751512915

The George Felse Omnibus
Warner pbk £9.99 0751510319

OTHERS

The Assize of the Dying
Headline pbk £4.99 0747236453

City of Gold and Shadows
Headline pbk £5.99 074723227X

Death Mask
Headline pbk £4.99 0747233721

Death to the Landlords
Headline pbk £4.50 0747231222

The Detective Omnibus
Headline pbk £7.99 0747240205

The Dominic Felse Omnibus
Headline pbk £9.99 0747237719

Flight of a Witch
Headline pbk £4.99 0747235562

The Funeral of Figaro
Headline pbk £4.99 0747233713

Holiday with Violence
Headline pbk £5.99 0747239231

The Horn of Roland
Headline pbk £4.99 0747236003

Mourning Raga
Headline pbk £4.99 0747231214

Never Pick Up Hitch-Hikers
Headline pbk £5.99 0747238405

The Piper on the Mountain
Headline pbk £4.99 0747232261

The Will and the Deed
Headline pbk £5.99 0747235708

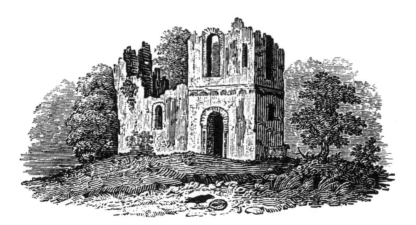

MIKE PHILLIPS

British crime writers have not always been as successful as their American counterparts in creating convincing narratives of life in the inner cities. Mike Phillips is one of the few who has. His series of books about the black journalist Sam Dean and his adventures on the meaner streets of London have an authenticity and a social incisiveness which are compelling. They deserve to be widely read.

The Dancing Face
HarperCollins hbk £15.99
0002326299

An Image to Die For
HarperCollins pbk £5.99
0006496717

EDGAR ALLAN POE (1809-1849)

Although crime and detection have played a role in fiction since the time of the Ancient Greeks, the writer who is generally considered to have invented the modern detective story is Edgar Allan Poe. In *The Murders in the Rue Morgue*, published in 1841, *The Mystery of Marie Roget* and *The Purloined Letter*, Poe's so-called 'tales of ratiocination', he brought together the basic ingredients of the genre. In the hero of these tales, C. Auguste Dupin, he created a type of detective who has recurred in various guises from the 1840s to the present day. Dupin is an intellectual and eccentric amateur: he approaches the mysteries scientifically and methodically, he analyses clues unnoticed or misinterpreted by the police and he produces his solution with a flourish that is surprising both to the other characters in the story and to the reader. He is accompanied by his friend, the narrator, who is obligingly dim and unobservant, thus serving as a foil to Dupin's brilliance. The influence of these tales by Poe has been immense and the resemblance of a host of later detectives to the archetypal Dupin is clear.

Complete Tales and Poems
Penguin pbk £11.00 0140103848

Fall of the House of Usher and Other Tales
Penguin pbk £2.50 0140432914

Selected Tales
Oxford UP pbk £2.50 0192815229

A. J. QUINNELL

A. J. Quinnell has been writing complex and absorbing thrillers, set in the more exotic locations of the world, for many years. Some of his books, particularly the series featuring the hard-bitten ex-mercenary Creasy, cross that ill-defined boundary between the adventure thriller and the crime novel. However they are defined, these well-written and exciting novels deserve a wide readership.

Black Horn
Orion pbk £5.99 1857977327

Man on Fire
Orion pbk £5.99 0752806343

Message from Hell
Orion pbk £5.99 0752803638

The Perfect Kill
Orion pbk £5.99 0752806351

Siege of Silence
Orion pbk £5.99 0752802593

Snap Shot
Orion pbk £5.99 1857977483

IAN RANKIN

Ian Rankin's creation Inspector John Rebus is a flawed man. Like many fictional detectives he drinks too much, smokes too much and has a complex and unsettled love-life. He is moody, fond of dreadful puns and dedicated to a job that chews people up and spits them out as a messy pulp of emotions and neuroses. One of Rankin's achievements has been to create a character who, flaws and all, is admirable and believable. Another has been to place the character in a recognisable setting – contemporary Edinburgh, beyond what the tourists see. These deftly-plotted police procedurals, built around a convincing central character, are highly recommended.

Black and Blue
Orion pbk £8.99 0752805150

The Black Book
Orion pbk £4.99 1857974131

Let it Bleed
Orion pbk £4.99 0752804014

Mortal Causes
Orion pbk £4.99 1857978633

Strip Jack
Orion pbk £4.99 0752809563

JULIAN RATHBONE

Born in 1935, Julian Rathbone is a versatile novelist whose work has twice been shortlisted for the Booker Prize. He is also a gifted exponent of crime and thriller fiction who uses the genre to investigate political and social issues, from ecological hazards to the threats of a post-Cold War world, in original and stylish novels.

Accidents Will Happen
Serpent's Tail pbk £8.99
1852423129

Sand Blind
Serpent's Tail pbk £7.99
1852422815

DEREK RAYMOND

A legendary and unique figure among British crime writers, Raymond pulled off the unsettling trick of resembling a character from one of his own books. Following a period of some success, or rather notoriety, as the author of a handful of lowlife London novels written under his real name (Robin Cook), Raymond enjoyed a spell of 'drifting' before he started writing crime fiction. With an irony he no doubt found hilarious, he was asked to change his name after the arrival of another Robin Cook, author of several successful medical thrillers. Perhaps this change of identity was just what he needed because Raymond, under his new name, published a series of excellent detective novels, all set in the seedy environs of the London underworld and all featuring a nameless policeman known only as the Detective Sergeant, Soho's answer to Dashiell Hammett's Continental Op. Specialising in casual displays of horrific violence, their pages littered with garish characters, the 'Factory' novels, as they're called, are superb, chilling examples of a particularly English hard-boiled crime fiction. Revered in France, where he lived for eighteen years and where his work has been filmed, Raymond returned to London to write *I Was Dora Suarez*, one of the most gruesome books ever published. He died in 1994 following the completion of an autobiographical work *The Hidden Files*. Always a disturbing talent, he deserves to be read by those of a strong disposition and a love of sincerity and savagery.

The Crust on its Uppers
Serpent's Tail pbk £7.99 1852422688

The Devil's Home on Leave
Warner pbk £4.99 0751508055

He Died With His Eyes Open
Warner pbk £4.99 0751508047

How the Dead Live
Warner pbk £4.99 0751508039

I Was Dora Suarez
Warner pbk £4.99 0751508063

Not Till The Red Fog Rises
Warner pbk £4.99 0751516228

A State of Denmark
Serpent's Tail pbk £8.99 1852423153

SAM REAVES

Praised by Robert B. Parker as 'too good. He makes me nervous.', Chicago-based Reaves is a writer who seems to have sprung from nowhere. His first novel, *A Long Cold Fall*, reads as if its author had been turning out tough guy thrillers for years. His protagonist Cooper MacLeish, a Vietnam vet now driving a cab around the Windy City, is a classic hard-boiled hero. Hardened by his past, yet with a big heart and a nice line in one-liners, Cooper could have stepped from the pages of Dashiell Hammett. In each of the books his efforts to help someone throw him into a world of danger and violence. In the first he's trying to reclaim his lost son and investigate the suspicious death of the boy's mother. *Fear Will Do It*, the second book, sees Cooper trying to extricate Diana, his girlfriend, from a tangle involving blackmail, drug smuggling and, inevitably, murder. In *Bury It Deep* Cooper is helping a journalist pal uncover a big scandal involving corrupt politicians. Soon they're both trying to stay alive as violence explodes around them. In *Get What's Coming* Cooper has settled down, married Diana and given up cabbying for a soft job as a chauffeur. When his wealthy boss's son is killed in a nightclub owned by his father, the police assume it was just another drug deal gone sour. Cooper thinks otherwise and sets out to prove it, even though this stands to cost him his job, his marriage and, possibly, his life. Crime fans are strongly recommended to take Robert B. Parker's advice and go on a tour of Cooper MacLeish's Chicago.

Bury It Deep
Headline pbk £5.99 0747253161

Fear Will Do It
Serpent's Tail pbk £7.99 1852423102

Get What's Coming
Headline pbk £5.99 0747253153

A Long Cold Fall
Serpent's Tail pbk £7.99 1852422394

> **'Have you found any- one yet? I mean, have you got any clues to who it was that – did it?'**
>
> **Ruth Rendell,**
> **Kissing the Gunner's Daughter**

RUTH RENDELL

Over the last decade Ruth Rendell has firmly established her position as one of this country's most prolific and most original writers of crime and suspense fiction. The sheer range of her work is impressive. She is equally at home with traditional crime fiction, in which a central detective investigates and unravels a murder mystery, and with novels in which the tension rests on the psychological dramas enacted by the chief protagonists. The seventeen novels featuring the stolid and dependable Chief Inspector Wexford and the provincial town of Kingsmarkham are superbly constructed, contemporary whodunnits which provide the customary satisfactions of an ingeniously worked out plot. Her non-Wexford novels are, if anything, even more rewarding. These books often deal brilliantly and disturbingly with odd, misfit characters and unusual behaviour, with families torn apart by love, hate and interdependency, with the passions hidden behind the facades of everyday life. Her novels can often stretch the limits of the genre to thought-provoking effect and she has been the recipient of many literary awards, including the CWA Diamond Dagger for work which has made a significant contribution to crime-writing. She has also written a number of novels under the pseudonym of Barbara Vine.

WEXFORD NOVELS

The Best Man to Die
Arrow pbk £4.99 0099259109

From Doon with Death
Arrow pbk £4.99 0099203502

A Guilty Thing Surprised
Arrow pbk £4.99 0099235005

Kissing the Gunner's Daughter
Arrow pbk £4.99 0099233819

Murder Being Once Done
Arrow pbk £4.99 0099073900

A New Lease of Death
Arrow pbk £4.99 0099259206

No More Dying Then
Arrow pbk £4.99 0099074001

Put on by Cunning
Arrow pbk £4.99 0099277301

Road Rage
Hutchinson hbk £15.99 0091792304

Shake Hands for Ever
Arrow pbk £4.99 0099129108

Simisola
Arrow pbk £5.99 0099437317

A Sleeping Life
Arrow pbk £4.99 0099199807

Some Lie and Some Die
Arrow pbk £4.99 0099092808

The Speaker of Mandarin
Arrow pbk £4.99 0099328100

An Unkindness of Ravens
Arrow pbk £4.99 0099328100

The Veiled One
Arrow pbk £4.99 0099602806

Wolf to the Slaughter
Arrow pbk £4.99 0099277409

Wexford : An Omnibus
Arrow pbk £9.99 0099566400

The Second Wexford Omnibus
Arrow pbk £9.99 0099666405

The Third Wexford Omnibus
Arrow pbk £9.99 0099803305

The Fourth Wexford Omnibus
Arrow pbk £9.99 0099848007

OTHERS

Blood Lines
Arrow pbk £4.99 0099887908

The Bridesmaid
Arrow pbk £4.99 0099681803

Collected Short Stories
Arrow pbk £9.99 0099546205

The Copper Peacock
Arrow pbk £4.99 0099928302

The Crocodile Bird
Arrow pbk £4.99 0099303787

A Demon in My View
Arrow pbk £4.99 0099148609

The Face of Trespass
Arrow pbk £4.99 0099106507

The Fallen Curtain
Arrow pbk £4.99 0099214601

The Fever Tree
Arrow pbk £4.99 0099321300

Going Wrong
Arrow pbk £4.99 0099808404

A Judgement in Stone
Arrow pbk £4.99 0099171406

The Keys to the Street
Arrow pbk £4.99 009918432X

The Killing Doll
Arrow pbk £4.99 0099399504

The Lake of Darkness
Arrow pbk £4.99 0099255308

Live Flesh
Arrow pbk £4.99 0099502704

Make Death Love Me
Arrow pbk £4.99 0099223309

Master of the Moor
Arrow pbk £4.99 0099304503

Means of Evil
Arrow pbk £4.99 0099299003

The New Girl-Friend
Arrow pbk £4.99 0099470306

One Across, Two Down
Arrow pbk £4.99 0099312603

The Secret House of Death
Arrow pbk £4.99 0099286602

Talking to Strange Men
Arrow pbk £4.99 0099535300

To Fear a Painted Devil
Arrow pbk £4.99 009920360X

The Tree of Hands
Arrow pbk £4.99 0099434709

Vanity Dies Hard
Arrow pbk £4.99 0099369206

The Ruth Rendell Omnibus
Arrow pbk £9.99 0099331713

The Second Ruth Rendell Omnibus
Arrow pbk £9.99 0099363011

ROBERT RICHARDSON

Richardson is a skilful and knowing modern exponent of the classic English detective story. His series hero, Augustus Maltravers, is a playwright and amateur detective who investigates murders and mysteries in such traditional settings as remote manor houses and peaceful cathedral closes. His first book, *The Latimer Mercy,* won the CWA Best First Novel Award in 1985. Richardson has also written novels outside the series which move more ambitiously beyond the conventions within which the Maltravers books operate.

Bellringer Street
Gollancz pbk £3.50 057504716X

The Book of the Dead
Gollancz pbk £3.50 0575048883

The Dying of the Light
Gollancz pbk £3.50 0575050918

The Hand of Strange Children
Gollancz pbk £4.99 0575057041

The Latimer Mercy
Gollancz pbk £3.99 057504537X

The Lazarus Tree
Gollancz pbk £3.99 0575055227

Significant Others
Gollancz pbk £5.99 0575600497

MIKE RIPLEY

Mike Ripley is one of the wittiest crime novelists now writing. His Angel novels, in which the streetwise Roy Angel undertakes a series of investigations in the dodgier areas of contemporary London's black economy, are full of cherishable one-liners and have twice won the CWA's Last Laugh Award for Funniest Crime Novel of the Year. Ripley has also written short stories and scripts for radio and television and has worked as crime fiction critic for *The Daily Telegraph*. As fellow crime novelist Val McDermid has remarked, 'If laughter is the best medicine, Mike Ripley's Angel novels should be on National Health prescription.'

Angel City
HarperCollins pbk £4.99 0006490123

Angel Confidential
HarperCollins pbk £4.99 0006496989

Angel Hunt
HarperCollins pbk £3.50 0006470963

Angel Touch
HarperCollins pbk £3.50 0006179118

Angels in Arms
HarperCollins pbk £4.99 000647263X

Family of Angels
HarperCollins pbk £5.99 0006498388

Just Another Angel
HarperCollins pbk £3.50 0006177603

That Angel Look
The Do-Not Press pbk £8.00 1899344233

CANDACE ROBB

Candace Robb, a scholar of medieval history and literature, has written a lively series of historical whodunnits set in fourteenth century England. Their protagonist is Owen Archer, an engaging one-eyed Welshman who was once captain of the archers for the Duke of Lancaster. The old Duke dies in 1363 and Owen becomes a sometime spy and detective for the Archbishop of York. Robb's great strengths as a writer of historical crime fiction are her attention to detail and her familiarity with the everyday routines of medieval life. Her imaginative recreation of lives lived to a rhythm of the seasons, and days ordered by the cadences of church and cathedral is convincing, and her detailed reconstruction of medieval York, as the setting for her stories, will delight the many who know that city.

The Apothecary Rose
Mandarin pbk £5.99 074931883X

The King's Business
Mandarin pbk £5.99 074931981X

The Lady Chapel
Mandarin pbk £5.99 0749318848

The Nun's Tale
Mandarin pbk £5.99 0749319828

The Riddle of St. Leonard's
Mandarin pbk £5.99 0749323655

SAX ROHMER (1886-1959)

Under his pseudonym Sax Rohmer, the English journalist and novelist Arthur Sarsfield Ward wrote a series of stories about the inscrutable and sinister Chinese criminal genius Fu Manchu, which were published over a period of nearly fifty years, from his first appearance in 1912 to *Emperor Fu Manchu* in 1959. The character also appeared in dozens of movies, radio programmes and TV episodes. To modern readers Fu Manchu embodies, with almost laughable obviousness, Western fears of Asian power and influence, of the encroaching 'yellow peril', but Rohmer's gifts for breathless and unself-conscious narrative make the stories readable still.

The Fu Manchu Omnibus Volume One
Allison & Busby pbk £8.99 0749002719

The Fu Manchu Omnibus Volume Two
Allison & Busby pbk £9.99 0749002220

KATE ROSS

Some periods of history are well supplied with fictional detectives. There are, for example, plenty of medieval mystery solvers and plenty of Victorian sleuths. Some periods are less over populated by amateur investigators. Kate Ross had the excellent idea of setting her well-written and thoroughly researched books in the era just before Victoria's accession to the throne and her novels featuring the Regency dandy and detective Julian Kestrel have won much praise for their originality.

Broken Vessel
Hodder pbk £5.99 0340628103

Cut to the Quick
Hodder pbk £5.99 0340609745

The Devil in Music
Hodder hbk £15.99 0340649259

Whom the Gods Love
Hodder pbk £5.99 0340649240

JAMES SALLIS

One of the finest of modern cult writers, Sallis first emerged in 1967 as a dazzling practitioner of new wave Science Fiction. His importance as a noir writer has become increasingly clear in the few years since the publication of *The Long-Legged Fly*. Readers of James Lee Burke will find an affinity with Sallis since his novels are set in New Orleans, only a few bayous away from the New Iberia of Burke's Dave Robicheaux series. Readers of Walter Mosley will be interested to compare the ways a black protagonist is treated by a white Texan writer rather than a black Californian. However Sallis has a unique take on Louisiana and Detective Lew Griffin, his guilt-ridden ex-alcoholic hero, is a creation at least as intriguing as Easy Rawlins. Writing with originality and style, Sallis brings a subtly postmodern sensibility to hardboiled noir. He experiments with non-linear plotting, resolves Lew Griffin's cases mid-book and plays challenging games with the notions of author, narrator and the reliability of first person storytelling. Yet he does all this so deftly that this bold experimentation is unlikely to alienate more traditional readers of noir fiction. Sallis is undoubtedly one of the most imaginative and innovative writers in the genre today.

Black Hornet
No Exit Press pbk £4.99
1874061637

Death Shall Have Your Eyes
No Exit Press pbk £4.99
1874061785

The Long-Legged Fly
No Exit Press pbk £4.99
1874061483

Moth
No Exit Press pbk £4.99
1874061521

LAWRENCE SANDERS

Author of several novels featuring his debonair sleuth Archy McNally, Sanders has had enormous success in America. Set in Palm Beach, his books are vastly entertaining and each one has a generous helping of suspense. Working for his lawyer father as an investigator, and aided and abetted by Binky Watrous, an accomplice of less than genius I.Q., McNally strolls urbanely through the books, with a drink and a glamorous woman usually to hand. Crime in the shape of blackmail, robbery and/or murder unsurprisingly raises its inelegant head, but Archy usually manages to sort things out before cocktail hour. Managing somehow to bridge the huge gap between P. G. Wodehouse and Carl Hiaasen, Sanders has mined a rich vein in the McNally novels. Each of the books has its own delights but the most recent in paperback, *McNally's Puzzle*, is as ingenious and enjoyable as any, centring on a typically improbable plot involving a missing mynah bird.

McNally's Caper
Hodder pbk £5.99 0340628790

McNally's Gamble
Hodder hbk £16.99 0340695293

McNally's Luck
Hodder pbk £4.99 0340592419

McNally's Puzzle
Hodder pbk £5.99 034067234X

McNally's Risk
Hodder pbk £5.99 0340604379

McNally's Secret
Hodder pbk £4.99 0340580208

McNally's Trial
Hodder pbk £5.99 0340639563

DOROTHY L. SAYERS (1893–1957)

Good writing can always survive changes in moral and social values and, in the right hands, crime writing, a much-maligned genre, can be a fine art. The witty and elegant novels of Dorothy L. Sayers continue to demonstrate the delicate skill involved in combining a compelling mystery with literary depth and flair. Some modern readers find Lord Peter Wimsey, her exquisitely sardonic and dilettante detective, to be infuriatingly snobbish and chauvinistic. Most recognise that, under the Wodehousian exterior, he is a complex character and one of the more convincing heroes of the classic age of detective fiction. His relationship with Harriet Vane, far from being chauvinistic, represented a revolutionary departure for the crime novel. Harriet is first introduced in *Strong Poison* in which Wimsey is trying to clear her of the accusation that she murdered her lover. Sayers's treatment of the relationship between Wimsey and Vane, in this and later novels, and her obvious sympathy for the latter, who is seen to be on trial largely because she is unconventional and female, does much to reveal the moral hypocrisy of the era. Sayers, who was also a translator of Dante and a writer on theology, was unashamedly intelligent and often ruthless in her clear-sighted analysis of people, class and society. Her detective stories, although dated in many ways, remain highly readable and her greatest gift may have been an ability to make what are almost novels of manners appealing to successive generations of popular fiction readers.

Busman's Honeymoon
Hodder pbk £5.99 0340489103

Clouds of Witness
Hodder pbk £4.99 0450001806

The Documents in the Case
Hodder pbk £4.99 0450002438

Five Red Herrings
Hodder pbk £4.99 0450012484

Gaudy Night
Hodder pbk £5.99 0450021548

Hangman's Holiday
Hodder pbk £5.99 0450019608

Have His Carcase
Hodder pbk £5.99 0450027120

In the Teeth of the Evidence
Hodder pbk £4.99 0450002489

Lord Peter Views the Body
Hodder pbk £5.99 0450017095

Murder Must Advertise
Hodder pbk £5.99 0340502177

The Nine Tailors
Hodder pbk £5.99 0450001008

Striding Folly
Hodder pbk £5.99 0450033406

Strong Poison
Hodder pbk £5.99 0450013928

Unnatural Death
Hodder pbk £5.99 0450001016

The Unpleasantness at the Bellona Club
Hodder pbk £5.99 0340502223

Whose Body
Hodder pbk £4.99 0450031292

SANDRA SCOPPETTONE

Some of the best crime fiction in America today is being written by women. Sandra Scoppettone has been much acclaimed in the States and is beginning to gain a high reputation in this country. In lesbian private eye Lauren Laurano, who combines street-savvy detecting with an ability to trawl through cyberspace in search of evidence, she has created an original and daring detective.

Everything You Have Is Mine
Virago pbk £6.99 1853814792

I'll Be Leaving You Always
Virago pbk £5.99 1853816647

Let's Face the Music and Die
Virago pbk £5.99 1860493181

My Sweet Untraceable You
Virago pbk £5.99 1853818895

KATE SEDLEY

England during the Wars of the Roses was a treacherous place for everyone from king to peasant. Constant shifts and changes in loyalties led to political assassinations amongst the highest in the land while the retinue of servants and courtiers that followed a lord often paid the ultimate price of their lives for their master's misfortunes. Into this world Kate Sedley introduces her sleuth Roger the Chapman, a travelling jack-of-all-trades and pedlar, who has an uncanny knack for stumbling across murder and mystery. Told in an engaging first person narrative, the books bring to life the medieval world of Edward IV's reign. Sedley has a talent for using small detail to convey daily life in a time both exquisite and brutal. She also presents a sympathetic revisionist view of Richard III, who was the Duke of Gloucester during his brother's reign. His melancholy presence, both seen and unseen, flits through the pages of this fine historical crime series.

Death and the Chapman
Headline pbk £5.99 0747244847

The Eve of Saint Hyacinth
Headline pbk £5.99 074724930X

The Hanged Man
Headline pbk £5.99 0747243263

The Holy Innocents
Headline pbk £5.99 0747246653

The Plymouth Cloak
Headline pbk £5.99 0747244863

The Wicked Winter
Headline pbk £5.99 0747256314

LAWRENCE SHAMES

Lawrence Shames has written five novels set in Florida's Key
West. This background is as important for what it is not, as
much as for what it is. To the characters who come to Key West,
in Shames's novels, what it is not is North and specifically not
New York. Plots revolve around people moving South – from
grey cities, winter coats and the common cold to a place where
semi-nudity is essential, roller-blading in lycra shorts in
December is absolutely normal and where gardens grow in
imported soil spread over local coral. Because of its inherent
strangeness and difference, largely a matter of climate, Key
West is where Shames's characters go to change - either because
they wish to or because they have to. Most come from the same
background and find that when you belong to a prominent
Mafia family, leaving that background may not be as simple as
you would like. The FBI and family, friends and enemies alike,
collude to ensure that breaks with the past can never be clean.
Despite touching on serious themes, Shames's novels are essentially entertainments. The pace is consistently fast, descriptions
of Floridian exotica are interspersed with self-consciously
'Goodfellas'- style dialogue and plots veer, equally self-consciously, towards the screwball. True love is found while complicated scams either go to plan, if the nice mafiosi are involved,
or not, if they are not. The edge of pathos never becomes sentimentality and the mafia characters are never totally unthreaten-
ing. However serious investigation of organised crime is not
Shames's aim. What he has produced is a sequence of novels
which has its own particular place in the tradition of Florida-
based crime writing.

Florida Straits
Pan pbk £4.99 0330331493
Scavenger Reef
Pan pbk £4.99 0330331507
Sunburn
Pan pbk £5.99 0330343564
Tropical Depression
Pan pbk £5.99 0330343572

'Had he been mistaken
when he had thought
there was a man in the
car, behind the corpse?'

Georges Simenon, *The Mouse*

SIMON SHAW

Simon Shaw is an actor and
his blackly comic novels are
set in the bitchy, backbiting
world of theatre and showbiz.
The series features Philip
Fletcher - professional actor
and amateur murderer -
whose egotism and amorality
are wittily dissected. Books in
the series have twice won the
Crime Writers' Association's
Last Laugh Award for
Funniest Crime Novel of the
Year.

Bloody Instructions
Gollancz pbk £3.99 0575052422

The Company of Knaves
HarperCollins pbk £5.99
0006498299

Killer Cinderella
Gollancz pbk £3.99 0575050349

The Villain of the Earth
Gollancz pbk £4.99 0575058099

GEORGES SIMENON (1903 - 1989)

The immensely popular series of *policiers* featuring the solid,
pipe-smoking figure of Commissaire Jules Maigret have served
to link Georges Simenon inextricably with Paris and particularly
Montmartre. However Simenon was a Belgian and spent much
of his life travelling. He started writing young and produced
vast amounts of undistinguished commercial fiction before
moving on to more serious work in the late twenties. The first
Maigret novel (*The Death of Monsieur Gallet*) secured his reputation and he continued the series throughout the thirties. The
Maigret stories differ from previous detective fiction in that little emphasis is placed on the traditional deductive analysis of
motive and evidence; instead Maigret employs an instinctual
method, plunging himself into the milieu of the crime until the
solution ripens for him. Maigret's calm presence and gift for
empathy have made him a fictional detective who ranks along-
side Sherlock Holmes in stature and influence. Simenon also
wrote what he termed 'hard novels' – novella-length stories that
address psychological themes such as revenge, guilt and familial
conflict. Among the best of these are the confessional *The Man
Who Watched Trains Go By* and *The Snow Was Black* in which a
ruthless killer achieves expiation through his own torture and
death at the hands of the Gestapo. These brilliantly tense and
economic novels have also had an immeasurable influence on
later crime writers, particularly on the continent. Simenon was
a massively prolific author, with over two hundred novels and
countless stories to his name. His skill in producing evocative
thumbnail sketches of characters and places rarely wavers and
he is one of the greatest of suspense writers. André Gide regarded
him as 'perhaps the greatest truly novelistic novelist' in France.

*Simenon is not currently in print in Britain. Some Waterstone's shops
may stock French editions of his novels.*

DOROTHY SIMPSON

Dorothy Simpson's books are amongst the finest recent examples of the traditional English crime novel, in which the still waters of small communities are proved to run deep. Her likeable detective Inspector Thanet – from, unsurprisingly, Kent – is an unglamorous but methodical hero whose patient persistence unearths the secrets that other characters in the books hope to keep hidden. Dorothy Simpson is a past winner of the CWA Silver Dagger Award for her novel *Last Seen Alive*.

A Day for Dying
Warner pbk £5.99 0751513776

Dead by Morning
Warner pbk £4.99 0751512729

Dead on Arrival
Warner pbk £4.99 075151411X

Doomed to Die
Warner pbk £4.50 0751506133

Element of Doubt
Warner pbk £4.99 075150842X

Harbingers of Fear
Warner pbk £4.99 0751510815

Inspector Thanet Omnibus
Warner pbk £8.99 0751508101

Last Seen Alive
Warner pbk £4.99 075150906X

The Night She Died
Warner pbk £3.99 0747404321

No Laughing Matter
Warner pbk £4.99 0751501530

Puppet for a Corpse
Warner pbk £4.99 0751508756

Second Inspector Thanet Omnibus
Warner pbk £8.99 0751513962

Six Feet Under
Warner pbk £4.99 075151019X

Suspicious Death
Warner pbk £4.99 0751511730

Wake the Dead
Warner pbk £4.99 0751501425

JOSEF SKVORECKY

Skvorecky is a major Czech novelist who was forced into exile in the aftermath of the Soviet invasion of 1968 and subsequently lived in Canada, where he continued to publish his tragicomedies of life on both sides of the Iron Curtain. As a devotee of classic crime fiction Skvorecky has been drawn to the genre on a number of occasions, and has produced several ironic variations on detective themes, mostly featuring the sad and slightly bewildered police lieutenant Boruvka. *Sins for Father Knox* is an ingenious collection of stories in which each of the tales violates one of the rules for crime fiction elaborated by the English crime writer Father Ronald Knox in his Detective Story Decalogue.

The End of Lieutenant Boruvka
Faber pbk £4.99 0571161626

The Mournful Demeanour of Lieutenant Boruvka
Faber pbk £5.99 0571149723

The Return of Lieutenant Boruvka
Faber pbk £4.99 057116420X

Sins for Father Knox
Faber pbk £4.99 057114313X

GILLIAN SLOVO

The greatest strength of Gillian Slovo's detective fiction is her protagonist and narrator Kate Baeier, a tough and feisty private investigator turned journalist who has suffered her fair share of personal tragedy. Socialist, feminist and saxophonist, Baeier is a woman of independent and strongly-held views and the action in the books is seen from her witty and humane perspective. The settings of the novels are convincingly contemporary and the plots explore issues which have significance outside the confines of genre fiction. In *Close Call*, for example, the starting point is police corruption. Baeier is back in London after five years abroad as a war correspondent. A routine profile for a glossy magazine leads her into a carefully orchestrated tale of hidden motives, drugs, blackmail and revenge for deeds twenty five years in the past. In all the novels Slovo provides crime stories which are well-paced and plotted, which have believable, witty and wise-cracking dialogue and which reflect the intelligence, integrity and love of life of the central character.

Cat Nap
Virago pbk £5.99 1853818151
Close Call
Virago pbk £5.99 185381816X
Death by Analysis
Women's Press pbk £6.99
0704345560
Death Comes Staccato
Women's Press pbk £6.99
0704340550
Ties of Blood
Headline pbk £5.99 0747233233

JOAN SMITH

Joan Smith works as a freelance writer and journalist, contributing witty and well-argued columns and articles to many national newspapers and magazines. She has also written *Misogynies*, a collection of essays on the theme of woman-hating and *Different for Girls*, an examination of the ways culture defines the differences between men and women. Smith's academic sleuth, Loretta Lawson, is a fully-rounded character – thoughtful, vulnerable, grouchy, full of doubts and a gutsy investigator. Loretta solves murders through a combination of tenacity and common sense and she even has her own Dr. Watson in the form of best friend Bridget Bennett. Every book is refreshingly good fun, filled with snappy dialogue and witty observation, as Loretta juggles her daily life with the complexities of murder investigations. Sophisticated and complex, Joan Smith's novels propel the reader forward at an exhilarating pace.

Don't Leave Me This Way
Faber pbk £5.99 0571161847
Full Stop
Vintage pbk £5.99 0099586312
A Masculine Ending
Faber pbk £5.99 0571151078
What Men Say
Vintage pbk £5.99 0099580012
Why Aren't They Screaming
Faber pbk £5.99 057115476X

MICKEY SPILLANE

At once unique and stereotypical, Mickey Spillane and his ruthless, amoral hero Mike Hammer represent the pulp tradition and its conventions taken to a level that is almost parody. Forever caught in the fifties of the Cold War, Hammer dishes out punishment to racketeers, gunmen and Commies (the three are often indistinguishable), wisecracks his way through blondes' boudoirs and knocks back the bourbon for breakfast. He also appears to be very nearly physically indestructible, recovering from wounds and beatings that would have put paid to lesser men. It is likely that Spillane and Hammer would have disappeared into that semi-oblivion that has been the fate of many pulp writers of the forties and fifties but films and TV were kind to them. Hammer has been filmed many times and the films include one cult masterpiece in Robert Aldrich's *Kiss Me Deadly*. A TV series starring Stacy Keach also kept him in the public eye. From the perspective of the nineties, Hammer is ludicrously macho and misogynist yet Spillane is an important figure in the history of crime fiction and, perhaps surprisingly, continues to publish. A new Hammer title, *Black Alley*, has just been published in the States. Spillane's writing, although it can hardly be regarded as stylish, is strangely compelling and he will survive as the ideal exemplar of fifties pulp writing.

The work of Mickey Spillane is not currently in print on the UK. Some larger Waterstone's branches may stock American editions of his novels.

VERONICA STALLWOOD

Many modern writers have taken the traditions and conventions of golden age crime fiction and re-worked them for a contemporary audience, to produce well-crafted and enjoyable mysteries. One of today's most acclaimed practitioners is Veronica Stallwood who has written a number of crime novels set in Oxford and featuring the novelist-cum-sleuth Kate Ivory. These highly readable and intelligent mysteries show why Mike Ripley in The Daily Telegraph described Stallwood as 'in the front rank of crime writers'.

Death and the Oxford Box
Headline pbk £5.99 0747244782
Deathspell
Headline pbk £5.99 0747257507
Oxford Exit
Headline pbk £5.99 0747248087
Oxford Fall
Headline pbk £5.99 074725513X
Oxford Mourning
Headline pbk £5.99 0747253439

RICHARD STARK

Richard Stark is the pseudonym of award-winning author Donald E. Westlake, a *nom-de-plume* which allows him to exercise the darker side of his imagination. Stark invented the professional thief Parker, tough, mean and spare, in prose to match and he was memorably portrayed by Lee Marvin in the 1967 film *Point Blank*. Most of the Parker novels have similar plots - Parker plans robbery, he and his team escape with the money, a double cross or fateful accident occurs, Parker loses money, Parker sets about regaining money, killing anyone who hinders him - but Stark's attention to detail in devising the robberies and in describing the intricacies of their planning give each book distinction. And then there is the character of Parker himself. He is a cold and ruthless killer, yet he holds the reader's attention. There is nobody else like him in crime fiction. The Parker novels are tense, terse and violent but they are gripping and exceptionally readable.

The Green Eagle Score
Allison & Busby pbk £3.95 0850317517
The Handle
Allison & Busby pbk £3.95 0850318149
The Mourner
Allison & Busby pbk £3.95 085031769X
The Parker Omnibus
Allison & Busby pbk £9.99 0749002395
Point Blank
Allison & Busby pbk £3.95 0850316731
The Rare Coin Score
Allison & Busby pbk £3.99 0850318718
Slayground
Allison & Busby pbk £5.99 0749000031
The Sour Lemon Score
Allison & Busby pbk £5.99 0749000295

STAYNES & STOREY

Over the last few years Jill Staynes and Margaret Storey have worked in partnership to produce a highly entertaining series of detective stories featuring Superintendent Bone. These witty mysteries, firmly in the classic tradition of English detective fiction, offer an enjoyable mix of high comedy and genuine suspense.

Bone Idle
Headline pbk £4.99 0747243271

Dead Serious
Headline pbk £4.99 0747250499

Goodbye, Nanny Gray
Headline pbk £4.99 0747250510

Grave Responsibility
Headline pbk £4.50 0747241074

A Knife at the Opera
Headline pbk £4.99 0747250502

The Late Lady
Headline pbk £4.99 0747241112

REX STOUT (1886–1975)

In a long career Rex Stout wrote many novels, both within the crime genre and outside it, but he is best remembered for the series of books featuring the mountainous gourmet Nero Wolfe. Wolfe, a man of abrasive wit and many eccentricities, is too slothful to leave the confines of his apartment, except on very rare occasions, but solves the crimes presented to him with the assistance of his encyclopedic intelligence and the legwork of his likeable sidekick, Archie Goodwin. The Nero Wolfe mysteries, written over many decades, are all well-written and erudite and have a particular charm of their own.

Even in the Best Families
Warner pbk £3.99 074740948X

If Death Ever Slept
Warner pbk £4.50 0751501670

More Deaths Than One
Warner pbk £4.50 0747409463

DOUG J. SWANSON

Hot on the heels of fellow Texan Joe R. Lansdale comes Doug
Swanson, a recent addition to the ranks of American crime writers. Whereas Lansdale writes of the more rural setting of East
Texas, Swanson bases his central character, private investigator
Jack Flippo, in Dallas. Armed with a dry wit, jaded, but
resourceful and likeable, Jack is a quintessential private eye.
Swanson's first novel, *Big Town*, has echoes of other crime
writers but has its own originality in its cleverly constructed
dialogue and in Flippo's laconic one-liners. A gripping tale of
murder and mayhem, perpetrated by as gruesome a gallery of
white trash misfits as ever lurched across a page, *Big Town* won
the John Creasey Memorial Award for best first crime novel.
Dreamboat consolidated the success of the first book and is set in
Lansdale's territory of East Texas. In what seems a simple insurance investigation, Jack is soon up to his neck in murder, surrounded by a cast of outrageous hillbilly psychos to make life
more exciting. *96 Tears,* the latest novel, has Jack back in Dallas
and trying to earn a relatively honest dollar. Stalkers, a wealthy
woman with a murky past and an old sparring partner from *Big
Town,* the hysterically appalling Teddy Tunstra, all conspire to
make his job an impossible one and soon his main concern is
staying alive. Swanson's three novels so far have shown that a
major new talent has emerged in American crime writing.

96 Tears
Warner pbk £5.99 075152008X

Big Town
Warner pbk £4.99 0751512478

Dreamboat
Warner pbk £5.99 0751515841

JULIAN SYMONS (1912–1994)

Julian Symons was a distinguished anthologist, critic and biographer as well as crime writer. His novels of the fifties added a psychological depth to crime fiction which had rarely been achieved before but he was also capable of wit, light-heartedness and knowledgeable pastiche in works featuring the thespian detective Sheridan Haynes, who specialises in the role of Sherlock Holmes on stage, and finds himself embroiled in Doyle-like mysteries off it. Symons was also the author of *Bloody Murder*, a valuable history of the genre, and was awarded the CWA Diamond Dagger in 1990 for his contribution to crime fiction.

The Advertising Murders
Pan pbk £4.99 0330322664

Bloody Murder
Pan pbk £4.50 0330333038

Death's Darkest Face
Pan pbk £4.50 0330315102

Playing Happy Families
Pan pbk £4.99 033033350X

Something Like a Love Affair
Pan pbk £4.99 0330328395

A Sort of Virtue
Pan pbk £5.99 0330350242

'It sometimes amuses me to embroider the plain cloth of fact with the golden thread of fancy.'

Julian Symons, *The Progress of a Crime*

ANDREW TAYLOR

Andrew Taylor has been a full-time writer for many years and has written books for younger readers and espionage thrillers, as well as crime fiction. This latter has been highly acclaimed and he won the John Creasey Memorial Award for his first novel. He has since been shortlisted for the CWA Gold Dagger. Perhaps his most interesting works are his tense and often shocking psychological thrillers. *The Barred Window* is a subtle investigation of a strange, symbiotic relationship between two cousins, told by an unreliable narrator who slowly reveals the darker secrets of the past. *The Four Last Things* is the first volume in an ambitiously planned trilogy - part crime fiction, part gothic melodrama – which will be published over the next couple of years.

An Air That Kills
Hodder pbk £5.99 0340617136

The Barred Window
HarperCollins pbk £5.99
0006472133

The Four Last Things
HarperCollins hbk £15.99
0002325578

The Lover of the Grave
Hodder hbk £16.99 0340617128

A Mortal Sickness
Hodder pbk £5.99 0340617144

JOSEPHINE TEY (1897–1952)

Josephine Tey was the pseudonym of Elizabeth Mackintosh, born in the Scottish Highlands, who had a distinguished career both as a crime novelist and as a playwright. Her plays are now largely forgotten but her crime fiction continues to be widely read. Her first novel, *The Man in the Queue,* introduced Inspector Alan Grant, the debonair and cerebral detective who would appear in four further classic mysteries - *The Daughter of Time, The Singing Sands, A Shilling for Candles* and *To Love and Be Wise.* Probably her best known book is *The Daughter of Time,* an intriguing blend of historical research, political thriller and crime novel. Convalescing in hospital, Inspector Grant ruminates on a portrait of Richard III, the hunchbacked villain of English history. He begins to doubt if Richard really did murder his nephews to secure the throne. Grant makes an imaginative leap into the political intrigues of the 1480s and, using his considerable powers of detection, he pieces together an alternative solution to the infamous case of the murder of the Princes in the Tower. In her other novels Tey reveals both a strong grasp of narrative and a deep understanding of character and the darker side of human nature which often moves beyond the apparent confines of traditional crime fiction. Her skilful plotting, incisive prose and meticulously researched settings are rarely matched by any but a few of her contemporaries.

The Daughter of Time
Mandarin pbk £5.99 0749310936

The Franchise Affair
Penguin pbk £5.99 0140128204

The Man in the Queue
Mandarin pbk £4.99 074931060X

Miss Pym Disposes
Mandarin pbk £4.99 0749310626

A Shilling for Candles
Mandarin pbk £4.99 0749310952

To Love and Be Wise
Mandarin pbk £4.99 0749310618

ROSS THOMAS

Something of a cross between Elmore Leonard and Graham Greene, Ross Thomas is an excellent writer with an array of impressive novels behind him. Certainly he deserves to be better known in this country. Perhaps he's not as popular as he should be because his books straddle the two genres of espionage novel and mystery novel. However they are just as full of suspense as any detective yarn and a lot more entertaining than most. Two characters stand out amongst the many he has created - Artie Wu and Quincy Durant who together comprise the investigative agency Wudu Ltd. The two books that feature them – *Out on the Rim* and *Voodoo Ltd* – are among the best examples of his compelling and often hilarious style. Twice winner of the Edgar Allan Poe award (US crime fiction's answer to the Oscar), Thomas is a writer crying out for more exposure on this side of the Atlantic. Even his titles (*Missionary Stew,* The *Fools in Town Are on Our Side, The Seersucker Whipsaw*) are great and the contents are even better.

Ah, Treachery
Warner pbk £5.99 0751515957

Twilight at Mac's Place
Warner pbk £4.50 0708852394

Voodoo Ltd
Warner pbk £4.99 075150078X

JIM THOMPSON (1906–1977)

Just before he died in 1977, at the age of 71, Jim Thompson claimed that one day his books would be regarded as classics of crime literature. At the time all of Thompson's twenty nine novels, which were written and published as cheap 'paperback originals', complete with garish and lurid covers, seemed to deny their creator's assertion. Thompson's reputation as a heavy drinker who told wild stories about his own background meant that few in literary circles paid any heed to his statement. A year after his death none of Thompson's books was in print in America or the UK. Reading Thompson today, it is difficult to believe that he was not immediately recognised as a master of the noir crime novel. His vision of a small town America peopled by sophisticated hustlers, dim-witted police officers, corrupt politicians, psychopathic bar-owners and neurotic drunks is uniquely compelling. Everybody is driven to fulfil their own desires and moral and social constraints are observed only for the sake of appearances. His chief protagonists move through the grim world he has created in search of their small chance of redemption, forever on the verge of that moment of self knowledge that will alter their behaviour. Thompson's greatest skill is to keep the reader uncertain, to the last page, whether that self-knowledge will be attained, that moment of redemption reached or the story will unfold with relentless fatality. The other key to the power of his writing is the ferocious intensity of his characterisation. He *was* his characters and, as one reads, one feels the raw anguish that his people, and Thompson, felt. In Britain Thompson's novels are being reissued and in America they are now all available and hailed as masterpieces. It is fitting that the prophecy of this troubled but brilliant writer has finally come true.

The Alcoholics
Vintage, USA pbk £6.50
0679733132

The Criminal
Vintage, USA pbk £5.99
0679733140

The Grifters
Vintage, USA pbk £6.99
0679732489

Jim Thompson Omnibus
Picador pbk £8.99 0330342886

Recoil
Vintage, USA pbk £6.99
0679733086

Second Jim Thompson Omnibus
Picador pbk £8.99 033034451X

South of Heaven
Vintage, USA pbk £7.99
0679740171

The Transgressors
Vintage, USA pbk £5.99
0679740163

Wild Town
Vintage, USA pbk £6.99
0679733124

MARK TIMLIN

Timlin is the author of fourteen novels featuring private investigator Nick Sharman, all of them set in the meanish streets of South London. Recently televised, the books bare a passing resemblance to the novels of fellow Londoner, the late Derek Raymond, and feature much of the violence of the latter's 'Factory' novels, if not quite the same sardonic wit. However they are a lively English equivalent of American hardboiled fiction, using the London locales very well, and Sharman is an engaging character - street wise and handy with a quip or two, tough if necessary but possessed of just enough sentiment to make the reader sympathetic.

Ashes by Now
Gollancz pbk £4.99 0575057831

Find My Way Home
Gollancz pbk £4.99 0575601760

A Good Year for the Roses
Headline pbk £5.99 0747234124

Gun Street Girl
Headline pbk £4.99 0747235090

Hearts of Stone
Headline pbk £5.99 0747238448

Paint It Black
Gollancz pbk £4.99 0575600144

Pretend We're Dead
Gollancz pbk £4.99 0575058285

Romeo's Tune
Headline pbk £4.99 0747234116

Sharman and Other Filth
Gollancz pbk £5.99 0575601019

A Street that Rhymed at 3 A.M.
Gollancz hbk £15.99 0575064056

Take the A-Train
Headline pbk £5.99 0747236992

The Turnaround
Headline pbk £4.99 0747237026

Zip Gun Boogie
Headline pbk £4.50 0747238030

PETER TREMAYNE

The popularity of historical crime fiction has meant the appearance in print of some fairly unlikely detectives, often clerical, operating in very nearly every period of history one could name. One of the most unlikely, and yet most engaging, is Peter Tremayne's Sister Fidelma, a 7th century Irish nun with a gift for unearthing the truth. As anthologist and critic Peter Haining has written, 'The Sister Fidelma stories take us into a world that only an author steeped in Celtic history could recreate so vividly – and one which no other crime novelist has explored before.'

Absolution by Murder
Headline pbk £5.99 0747246025

Shroud for the Archbishop
Headline pbk £5.99 0747248486

Spider's Web
Headline hbk £16.99 0747216525

The Subtle Serpent
Headline pbk £5.99 0747252866

Suffer Little Children
Headline pbk £5.99 0747248494

SCOTT TUROW

When Scott Turow published his first novel, *Presumed Innocent*, ten years ago it was given the sort of build-up that most first novelists can only dream about. Expectations were high before publication. This story of a chief prosecuting attorney, who is accused of a crime he has been instructed to solve, more than lived up to those expectations and the courtroom scenes had tension, drama and an authenticity that owed a lot to Turow's own experience as a prosecutor in the Chicago US Attorney's office. Since *Presumed Innocent*, Turow has published several more beautifully crafted legal thrillers set in Chicago and the Mid-West. The quiet, forceful intensity of his storytelling and his careful avoidance of contrivance and cliché give his books a stature unmatched by any other similar writer. His most recent title is *The Laws of Our Fathers* in which the shooting down of a respectable white woman in a run-down black ghetto is the starting point for a story which weaves back and forth from the present to the 1960s.

The Burden of Proof
Penguin pbk £5.99 0140138633

The Laws of Our Fathers
Penguin pbk £5.99 0140261850

Pleading Guilty
Penguin pbk £5.99 0140231080

Presumed Innocent
Penguin pbk £5.99 0140103368

ANDREW VACHSS

Andrew Vachss is as much a campaigner against a particular social ill as he is a writer. He is a lawyer in private practice specialising in juvenile justice and the unmasking of child abuse, and all his writings, novels and comics, fact and fiction, reflect this. Most of his novels focus on Burke and his extended family, all of whom have been damaged by some form of abuse and who live on the margins of society. Burke is not a conventional detective but, often through his extended family, he is drawn into cases where child abuse, deprivation and depravity are taking their toll of people's lives. Vachss is no literary stylist but his directness and supercharged language goes some way towards bringing home the full horror of his subject matter. Everything he writes about, he says, is based on truth. Indeed he claims to have toned down much of what he has witnessed. He has also written comic books, both original creations and publisher properties, and even these return to the subject of child abuse and reflect his passionate horror and indignation that a supposedly civilized society can tolerate such crimes in its midst.

Blossom
Pan pbk £4.50 033031873X
Blue Belle
Pan pbk £4.99 0330308807
Flood
Pan pbk £4.99 0330293249
Hard Candy
Pan pbk £5.99 0330316990
Sacrifice
Pan pbk £5.99 0330324144
Shella
Pan pbk £5.99 0330334131

BARBARA VINE

In her superb psychological thrillers Barbara Vine (Ruth
Rendell) employs perennial themes of revenge and remorse,
love and destructive hatred, to draw the reader in to the subtle
and detailed webs she spins in her plots. Absorbed by every
twist and surprise in the narrative, we are led through the maze
of events, past and present, towards the conclusion, which has
been implicit in them throughout the book, but which remains,
nonetheless, profoundly shocking. In the world of Barbara Vine
the capacity for evil pervades the fabric of everyday life and her
novels are logical explorations and investigations of everyone's
potential for wrongdoing and how circumstances sometimes
conspire to reveal it. Vine has created a body of work in which
suspense and atmosphere always play crucial roles. However
each of the novels has its own unique and disturbing identity. In
A Dark-Adapted Eye, the first of the eight books, a woman's
attempts to uncover family secrets reveals repressions still lurk-
ing behind respectable middle-clas facades. *In The House of
Stairs* happiness and liberation in the swinging sixties turn to
nightmare and murder. *The Brimstone Wedding* is a parallel tale
of two illicit loves, one contemporary and one in the past, and a
gradual description of how one led to tragedy. Parallel narratives, two or more perspectives on the same events, contrasts
and similarities between characters – Vine uses all these devices
and more to create the slowly smouldering suspense that gives
her books their distinct flavour. Her dense and engrossing
books are among the best examples not just of the psychological
thriller but of the contemporary novel.

Asta's Book
Penguin pbk £5.99 0140176616
The Brimstone Wedding
Penguin pbk £5.99 0140252800
Dark-Adapted Eye
Penguin pbk £5.99 0140086366
Fatal Inversion
Penguin pbk £5.99 0140086374
Gallowglass
Penguin pbk £5.99 0140132058
House of Stairs
Penguin pbk £5.99 0140114467
King Solomon's Carpet
Penguin pbk £5.99 0140156917
No Night Is Too Long
Penguin pbk £5.99 0140250409
Three Novels
Penguin pbk £9.99 0140138447

'And then she heard something drop with a heavy crash to the floor and looked. The shingle was still sliding down like sand in an hour-glass but now something big and heavy thudded to the ground. The gold, the gold: screamed Harvey.'

Edgar Wallace

EDGAR WALLACE (1875–1932)

The illegitimate son of an actress, Wallace was adopted by a Billingsgate fish-porter and grew up in the poorer streets of London. After a series of jobs Wallace found his metier as a journalist and worked as a Reuters correspondent in the early months of the Boer War before joining the *Daily Mail*. Due to his ingenuity the Mail was ale to headline the 1901 Peace treaty before even the government was officially informed of it. Kitchener immediately banned Wallace from every war front. Wallace took up fiction after a falling out with the *Mail* and, in doing so, became one of Britain's most prolific thriller writers, producing a huge number of novels and short stories for magazines and newspapers. It has been claimed that, in the twenties, one in four books sold was by Edgar Wallace. The full extent of Wallace's prodigous output may never be known since many of the serialisations were not published in book form. *The Road to London*, for example, only appeared in book form in 1986 after being discovered by a researcher in a twenties magazine and ther must be much more Wallace material hidden in newspaper and magazine archives. Wallace worked mostly in the realm of cliche and stereotype. Classic Wallace contains a beautiful and usually rich heroine, a mysterious young man who is not all that he seems and an eccentric villain who heads a gang of homicidal thugs. Yet some of his characters do achieve a certain stature and memorability. In the *Ringer* he created a classic anti-hero, a thief and a murderer who yet has his own moral code. And there is no denying Wallace's skill as a purveyor of unsophisticated but gripping narrative. He died in Hollywood in 1932 where he was working on the script of *King Kong*.

The Four Just Men
Oxford UP pbk £4.95 0192823884

MINETTE WALTERS

Minette Walters is still a relatively new voice in British crime fiction. Her highly assured debut novel *The Ice House* was published in 1992 to great critical acclaim. Despite modern settings and language, Walters is, in some important ways, a traditional crime novelist. She does not, for instance, choose to focus on the graphic details of the crimes or on the detailed forensic methods of a modern police investigation. Instead she concentrates on developing strong plots and complex characters whose lives are thrown into chaos by extraordinary events. These characters are shrewdly, often wryly, observed, with a great deal of psychological insight. Walters does break with one of the conventions of the genre. She has not chosen to create a central detective figure who moves from one novel to the next. One of the results of this is an urgency and immediacy about the novels which is refreshing – they take you by the throat and will not let you go. The books can be read in any order and each one stands in its own right as a complex mystery and engaging novel. Like all good crime writers Walters sows plenty of clues along the way and trails red herrings in about equal number. More often than not the reader is neatly wrong-footed. This works especially well, and to horrifying effect, in *The Dark Room*. The truth, when it finally dawns, is chilling, horrible and utterly convincing. Walters has written five novels so far and has already established herself as a major writer in the genre whose next work is eagerly awaited.

The Dark Room
Pan pbk £5.99 0330343742

The Echo
Macmillan pbk £9.99 0333713788

The Ice House
Pan pbk £5.99 0330327917

The Scold's Bridle
Pan pbk £5.99 0330336630

The Sculptress
Pan pbk £5.99 0330330373

JOSEPH WAMBAUGH

Having served fourteen years with the Los Angeles Police Force, Wambaugh is ideally suited to write about them and he has done so in a brilliant series of books. Although eclipsed recently by James Ellroy, Wambaugh is the more realistic writer, eschewing Ellroy's predilection for garish violence in favour of a grimly factual, though no less shocking, perspective. Ellroy's LAPD is a part (albeit a large one) of his attempt to rewrite Los Angeles history from the war years to the sixties. Essentially the police are another colourful ingredient, together with the politicians, racketeers, movie stars, hustlers and the rest of the Hollywood stew. For Wambaugh the LAPD is the whole thing, the rest of it the trimmings. Wambaugh's characters make up the rank and file of the force - no top brass, no district attorney, no heroes. These are just basic cops, with plenty of attitude, who do what is, in some cases, the best but, in most cases, the worst job in the world. Wambaugh's work also eloquently reflects the ethnic melting plot that is LA. Blacks, Irish, Mexicans, Japanese, all march through the books but skin colour is irrelevant once they don the blue-black uniform. *The Onion Field* is a powerful fictional recreation of a real-life cop-murder case. Of the other novels, all of which are worth reading, *The Choirboys* is particularly gripping. Savage, compelling and punctuated by moments of the darkest humour, it achieves admirably Wambaugh's aim of conveying to his readers something of the everyday realities of life as an LA cop.

The Choirboys
Warner pbk £4.99 0860074323

Finnegan's Week
Bantam pbk £4.99 0553407961

The Onion Field
Warner pbk £4.99 0860070891

PATRICIA WENTWORTH

(1878–1961)
Originally a writer of historical romances, Patricia Wentworth soon turned to mystery stories and she became one of the leading practitioners of the 'golden age' of English detective fiction. Her novels featuring the retired governess turned private investigator, Miss Maud Silver, with their complex, occasionally fantastic plots and their confident and competent narratives, retain their popularity.

The Alington Inheritance
Hodder pbk £5.99 0340682612

The Benevent Treasure
Hodder pbk £3.50 0340263733

The Brading Collection
Hodder pbk £5.99 0340672390

The Case Is Closed
Hodder pbk £5.99 0340200464

The Chinese Shawl
Hodder pbk £4.99 0340108991

The Clock Strikes Twelve
Hodder pbk £5.99 0340682620

The Girl in the Cellar
Hodder pbk £5.99 0340672404

Ivory Dagger
Hodder pbk £5.99 0340671653

The Listening Eye
Hodder pbk £3.99 0340217944

Out of the Past
Hodder pbk £5.99 0340671645

Poison in the Pen
Hodder pbk £3.99 0340217928

Spotlight
Hodder pbk £3.99 0340178337

DONALD E. WESTLAKE

Donald E. Westlake is one of America's most prolific crime novelists who has written over forty novels under his own name and many more under the pseudonym Richard Stark. His first novel *The Mercenaries*, the tale of a hit man torn between love and duty, was published in 1960 and was an instant hit with both the public and the Mystery Writers of America who awarded it their premier accolade. His hardboiled reputation was confirmed by *361* (1962) and *Killy* (1963), the story of the murderous consequences of a union's attempt to infiltrate a closed shop in a smalltown factory. However, despite the success of these early novels, populated by young men forced into violence and crime by forces beyond their control, Westlake is best known today for his range of comic crime novels. These are knockabout capers in which the characters are led into ever more ridiculous and improbable situations. A man impersonates his own brother in order to marry identical twin heiresses and ends up killing them both (*Too Much*). Two policemen supplement their income by undertaking robberies in the perfect disguise – as policemen (*Cops and Robbers*). The cream of the comic novels are the eight books featuring the hapless burglar John Dortmunder and his hand-picked team of dysfunctional accomplices. The plots are usually variations on a theme. Dortmunder is employed to steal a specific object – a rare emerald or, in one of the stories, the fossilised femur of a medieval saint. He steals it, loses it, steals it back again, loses it again, until a conclusion is reached and he is, usually, cheated out of his payment. These stylish and light-hearted entertainments are great fun and form just one part of Westlake's impressive and varied output.

Donald Westlake Omnibus
Allison & Busby pbk £7.99 0749002263

CHARLES WILLEFORD (1919 - 1988)

Charles Willeford was born in 1919 and, at various stages of his life, was a horse trainer, boxer, radio announcer, painter and tank commander at the Battle of the Bulge. Although he claimed that half the men he met in the army were like the psychopaths who people his later novels, he re-enlisted for another ten years when the war finished. When he finally left the army he settled in Miami, the city that provided the back-drop for many of his novels. His first crime novel *High Priest of California*, published in 1953, was highly acclaimed and was followed by *Pickup* (1954), the tale of a couple full of booze and despair which has a truly remarkable final twist. In the next thirty years, although not a prolific writer, Willeford wrote a number of other gritty, realistic novels, including *The Burnt Orange Heresy* and, most notably, *Cockfighter*, a disturbing story of a man obsessed by a cruel, bloody and illegal sport. 1984 saw the publication of *Miami Blues* and the first appearance of Sergeant Hoke Moseley, Willeford's most popular character. Solving cases through local Miami knowledge, occasional violence but, usually, sheer good fortune, Moseley cuts a sham-bolic figure – divorced, scruffy, resident of a seedy hotel, he is losing his hair and possessed of a set of cheap, blue-tinted false teeth. Moseley's character develops strongly in the four further novels Willeford published before his death in 1988.

Charles Willeford Omnibus
No Exit Press pbk £9.99 1874061394

Miami Blues
No Exit Press pbk £4.99 1874061564

New Hope for the Dead
No Exit Press pbk £4.99 1874061572

Sideswipe
No Exit Press pbk £4.99 1874061513

The Way We Die Now
No Exit Press pbk £4.99 187406170X

ROBERT WILSON

Robert Wilson has worked in shipping and trading in Africa and has drawn on his knowledge of the continent in his three engaging novels featuring Bruce Medway, fix-er and debt-collector to any-one in a deeper hole than himself in the murky com-mercial world of West Africa. The Medway novels are witty and fast-moving, the central character is a darkly wise-cracking anti-hero and the plots are peopled by a large supporting cast of dodgy and shady deal-makers, all in search of a quick buck. They are amongst the most origi-nal and readable British crime fiction to appear in the nineties.

The Big Killing
HarperCollins pbk £5.99
0006479863

Blood Is Dirt
HarperCollins hbk £15.99
0002326256

Instruments of Darkness
HarperCollins pbk £4.99
0006479855

R. D. WINGFIELD

The TV series starring David
Jason has done much to raise
the sales and profile of
Wingfield's books about the
crude, scruffy but effective
Detective Inspector Jack
Frost. The novels are entertainingly written police procedurals and the character of
Frost, although firmly within
the well-worn tradition of the
maverick cop who nonethe-
less gets results, is a genuinely
memorable creation.

Frost at Christmas
Transworld pbk £5.99 0552139815
Hard Frost
Transworld pbk £5.99 0552144096
Night Frost
Transworld pbk £5.99 0552145580
Touch of Frost
Transworld pbk £5.99 0552145556

MARY WINGS

Lesbian detective Emma
Victor made her first appearance in 1986 in *She Came Too
Late*. More 'She Came . . . '
thrillers followed, each as witty and hard-boiled as the last.
Wings's novels are brisk,
lavender renderings of the
classic noir novel which sub-
vert and then steal a genre
usually reserved for the boys.
Emma Victor is a resourceful,
relentless and inspiring heroine. The political message
and social conscience which
she embodies are perfectly
balanced by the fast pace of
the writing. Wings's plots are
tense, packed with intrigue
and, of course, there is the
inevitable love interest. In
1993 Wings won the Lambda
Literary Award with *Divine
Victim*, a Gothic detective novel which is one of her best.

Divine Victim
Women's Press pbk £5.99
0704343231
She Came By the Book
Women's Press pbk £5.99
0704344327
She Came in a Flash
Women's Press pbk £5.99
0704341085
She Came to the Castro
Women's Press pbk £6.99
070434520X
She Came Too Late
Women's Press pbk £5.99
0704339951

DANIEL WOODRELL

Born and bred in the Ozark mountains, Woodrell dropped out of school and joined the Marines when he was seventeen. After his period in the forces he studied intermittently at college, finally received his degree at the age of twenty seven and then spent two years at the prestigious Iowa Writers' Workshop. Since then Woodrell has published a number of novels and has been responsible for the creation of what he himself has called Country Noir, a heady concoction of white trash feuds and crimes, described in an extraordinarily rich and virtuoso prose style. His first book, *Under the Bright Lights*, introduces the reader to Rene Shade, the ex-prizefighter cajun cop who is the son of a legendary but elusive gambler, John X. Shade. The setting for the book is Frogtown, the cajun quarter of St. Bruno, Louisiana, where local gangster Auguste Beauraine maintains crime at a tolerable level and keeps the mayor happy. Only when outsiders upset the delicately controlled equilibrium do the mayor and his dodgy allies need someone to reinstate the rotten but manageable status quo and Shade is called in. Three further books have developed the characters of Shade, his siblings and his father, who returns to Frogtown in unexpected circumstances. Woodrell has also written *Woe to Live On*, an extraordinary novel set in the American Civil War, and *Give Us a Kiss*, in which Doyle Redmond, a down-at-heel writer, finds, like Rene Shade in the Frogtown books, that family loyalties and family histories lead him into brutal and unforgiving situations.

Give Us a Kiss
No Exit Press pbk £6.99 1874061645
Muscle for the Wing
No Exit Press pbk £5.99 1874061300
The Ones You Do
No Exit Press pbk £5.99 1874061203
Under Bright Lights
No Exit Press pbk £5.99 1874061319

CORNELL WOOLRICH (1903–1968)

Cornell Woolrich was the Poe of the pulp stands. Like Poe he led a miserable private life, haunted by alcoholism and repressed homosexuality; like Poe, he wrote stories which are terrifyingly ingenious, full of lurid incident and the sense of a malign universe; like Poe, his works found acclaim across the Atlantic in France, where his 'black' series of novels gave rise to the terms 'roman noir' and, ultimately, 'film noir'. Woolrich, who also wrote pseudonymously as William Irish and George Hopley, was no hard-boiled realist. If his typical protagonist is a lonely, big-city everyman who might have stepped out of a nightscape by Hopper, this only serves to heighten the suspense caused by his inevitable decent into a maelstrom of paranoia, obsession and cruel coincidence. His plot devices often defy credibility, but Woolrich's insistence on the 'line of suspense' keeps the reader hooked. It is no wonder that film-makers such as Hitchcock (*Rear Window*), Truffaut (*The Bride Wore Black*), Tourneur, Siodmak and many others have rushed to adapt his work. Woolrich was a prolific writer but it is in stories such as *Rear Window, Phantom Lady* and *I Married a Dead Man* that his uniquely tormented vision can be seen to best effect.

The novels of Cornell Woolrich are out of print in the UK. Some larger Waterstone's branches may stock American editions of his books.

MARGARET YORKE

Margaret Yorke is an experienced and talented writer who has been publishing crime fiction for many years. She began by producing an unexceptional, although entertaining, series featuring Inspector Patrick Grant. However the publication of *No Medals for the Major* in the seventies signalled a new direction for her writing. Although still a detective story, this novel is also a psychological study of a complex man and subsequent books have been similarly subtle in their characterisation. These novels are deeply involving – there is always much more at stake than discovering whodunnit and Yorke leads the reader into the centre of the psychological maelstrom which is generated when a brutal crime occurs. She is strict with pace, allowing the suspense to build gradually whilst also creating the momentum required to keep the reader fully engrossed. The air of tension heightens as the plots move on towards inevitably dramatic conclusions, conclusions which even the most seasoned addict of crime fiction will be hard pushed to second guess.

Act of Violence
Little Brown hbk £15.99
0316882542

Almost the Truth
Warner pbk £5.99 0751512168

The Cost of Silence
Warner pbk £4.99 0751511927

Crime in Question
Warner pbk £5.99 0751518573

Dangerous to Know
Arrow pbk £4.99 0099295512

No Medals for the Major
Warner pbk £4.99 0751511935

Pieces of Justice
Warner pbk £5.99 075151392X

The Point of Murder
Warner pbk £4.99 0751511943

A Question of Belief
Warner pbk £5.99 0751518506

Safely to the Grave
Warner pbk £5.99 0751516589

Serious Intent
Warner pbk £5.99 0751515965

A Small Deceit
Warner pbk £5.99 0751517720

The Small Hours of the Morning
Warner pbk £4.99 0751511919

Speak for the Dead
Warner pbk £5.99 0751516597

THE CRIME WRITERS' ASSOCIATION

The Crime Writers' Association was founded in 1953 by John Creasey and its membership now includes writers of all kinds of crime fiction, from historical crime to police procedurals, from true crime to thrillers. Its aim is to enhance the prestige and appreciation of crime-writing and to act as a professional body representing the interests of crime writers. The CWA gives a series of annual Dagger awards for excellence in crime writing which have long been recognised as the most important British awards in the field. These include awards for Best First Crime Novel of the Year (The John Creasey Memorial Dagger) and an award for funniest crime novel of the year (The CWA Last Laugh Dagger). However the major awards are the CWA Gold Dagger for Fiction, for the best crime novel of the year, and the CWA Diamond Dagger given to a writer who has made a significant contribution to crime-writing.

THE CWA GOLD DAGGER FOR FICTION – PAST WINNERS

1960 Lionel Davidson
The Night of Wenceslas

1961 Mary Kelly
The Spoilt Kill

1962 Joan Fleming
When I Grow Rich

1963 John Le Carré
The Spy Who Came in from the Cold

1964 H. R. F. Keating
The Perfect Murder

1965 Ross Macdonald
The Far Side of the Dollar

1966 Lionel Davidson
A Long Way to Shiloh

1967 Emma Lathen
Murder Against the Grain

1968 Peter Dickinson
Skin Deep

1969 Peter Dickinson
A Pride of Heroes

1970 Joan Fleming
Young Man I Think You're Dying

1971 James McClure
The Steam Pig

1972 Eric Ambler
The Levanter

1973 Robert Littell
The Defection of A. J. Lewinter

1974 Anthony Price
Other Paths to Glory

1975 Nicholas Meyer
The Seven Per Cent Solution

1976 Ruth Rendell
A Demon in my View

1977 John Le Carre
The Honourable Schoolboy

1978 Lionel Davidson
The Chelsea Murders

1979 Dick Francis
Whip Hand

1980 H. R. F. Keating
The Murder of the Maharajah

1981 Martin Cruz Smith
Gorky Park

1982 Peter Lovesey
The False Inspector Dew

1983 Joint Award
John Hutton
Accidental Crimes

Eric Wright
The Night the Gods Smiled

1984 B. M. Gill
The Twelfth Juror

1985 Paula Gosling
Monkey Puzzle

1986 Ruth Rendell
Live Flesh

1987 Barbara Vine
A Fatal Inversion

1988 Michael Dibdin
Ratking

1989 Colin Dexter
The Wench is Dead

1990 Reginald Hill
Bones and Silence

1991 Barbara Vine
King Solomon's Carpet

1992 Colin Dexter
The Way Through the Woods

1993 Patricia Cornwell
Cruel and Unusual

1994 Minette Walters
The Scold's Bridle

1995 Val McDermid
The Mermaids Singing

1996 Ben Elton
Popcorn

The CWA Diamond Dagger – Past Winners

1986 Eric Ambler
1987 P. D. James
1988 John Le Carre
1989 Dick Francis
1990 Julian Symons
1991 Ruth Rendell
1992 Leslie Charteris
1993 Ellis Peters
1994 Michael Gilbert
1995 Reginald Hill
1996 H. R. F. Keating

CRIME ANTHOLOGIES

There are many anthologies of crime writing and crime fiction available. This is a selection of a few of the best and most entertaining collections currently in print in this country.

Fresh Blood *ed. Mike Ripley and Maxim Jakubowski*
Do-Not Press pbk £6.99 1899344039
Fresh Blood II *ed. Mike Ripley and Maxim Jakubowski*
Do-not Press pbk £8.00 1899344209

These two volumes gather together the cream of Britain's new wave of crime writers, the new generation of writers whose fiction deals with real crime committed by real criminals. The first volume includes original short stories by Derek Raymond, Mark Timlin, Nicholas Blincoe, Stella Duffy, Ian Rankin and others. Amongst writers with work in the second volume are Charles Higson, Christopher Brookmyre, Ken Bruen, Lauren Henderson and John Williams.

London Noir *ed. Maxim Jakubowski*
Serpent's Tail pbk £8.99 1852423080

A collection of short crime stories which explore the darker side of London. Writers from Derek Raymond to Liza Cody tell tales of mayhem and depravity in the capital.

Mammoth Book of Historical Detectives *ed. Mike Ashley*
Robinson pbk £6.99 1854874063

These stories come from all over the world and from all historical periods and are written not only by such well-known authors as Ellis Peters and Robert Van Gulik but also by newcomers to the field of historical crime fiction. The detectives include such well-known characters from literary history as Hans Christian Andersen and, in Lillian De la Torre's superb stories (not readily available in this country), Dr. Samuel Johnson.

Mammoth Book of Pulp Fiction *ed. Maxim Jakubowski*
Robinson pbk £6.99 1854875078

This is an excellent collection of pulp offerings from the last seventy years, including work by Raymond Chandler, Dashiell Hammett, Ed Mc Bain and James Ellroy.

Orion Book of Murder *ed. Peter Haining*
Orion pbk £6.99 0752809156
Subtitled One Hundred of the World's Greatest Crime Stories, this is a full and
generous collection of mystery and crime tales by a wide variety of authors. Ruth
Rendell, Graham Greene, Ngaio Marsh, Colin Dexter, Ellery Queen, Conan Doyle
and P. D. James are just some of the authors included in the collection.

Oxford Book of American Detective Stories *ed. Tony Hillerman*
Oxford UP hbk £17.50 0195085817
This collection traces the development of the American detective story from Edgar
Allan Poe in the 1840s to Marcia Muller in the 1990s. This a varied anthology
which represents writers from a number of different periods and different geo-
graphical backgrounds.

Spooks, Spies and Private Eyes *ed. Paula L. Woods*
Payback Press pbk £7.99 0862416086
This is a rich and unprecedented collection of mystery, crime and suspense fiction
produced by black writers. Beginning with the classic locked-room mystery *Talma
Gordon* by Pauline Hopkins it ranges from the work of Chester Himes through
non-genre writers such as Richard Wright to modern masters like Walter Mosley
and Gar Anthony Harwood.

Victorian Detective Stories *ed. Michael Cox*
Oxford UP pbk £7.99 019283150X
An anthology which brings together 31 of the best tales of mystery and detection
from the Victorian era. Authors include Edgar Allan Poe, Baroness Orczy, Wilkie
Collins and Sax Rohmer.

AUTHORS BY SUB-GENRE

In the main body of the guide the authors are organised alphabetically by surname. Here we have grouped the same authors in broad sub-genres of crime writing. Some authors appear in more than one sub-genre. We know that, to some extent, the sub-genres are arbitrary and that writers do not fall so easily into such classifications. However we believe that grouping the writers in these very loose categories will help readers discover new authors whose novels they will enjoy and will help to navigate them through the enormous range of writing in the guide.

PIONEERS

Wilkie Collins
Conan Doyle
E. W. Hornung
Marie Belloc Lowndes
Edgar Allan Poe
Sax Rohmer
Edgar Wallace

GOLDEN AGE OF ENGLISH CRIME FICTION

Margery Allingham
E. C. Bentley
G. K. Chesterton
Agatha Christie
Edmund Crispin
Michael Gilbert
Michael Innes
Ngaio Marsh
Gladys Mitchell
Dorothy L. Sayers
Josephine Tey
Patricia Wentworth

GOLDEN AGE UPDATED

Catherine Aird
Robert Barnard
Kate Charles
Deborah Crombie
Colin Dexter
Elizabeth Ferrars
Antonia Fraser
Elizabeth George
Caroline Graham
Ann Granger
D. M. Greenwood
Martha Grimes
H. R. F. Keating
Emma Lathen
Janet Laurence
Peter Lovesey
Susan Moody
Ellis Peters
Robert Richardson
Dorothy Simpson
Veronica Stallwood
Staynes & Storey

Julian Symons
Margaret Yorke

BRITISH NOIR

Nicholas Blincoe
Christopher Brookmyre
Dan Kavanagh
Ted Lewis
Derek Raymond
Mark Timlin

MODERN BRITISH

Lesley Grant-Adamson
Jo Bannister
John Le Carré
Michael Dibdin
Lauren Henderson
Reginald Hill
Bill James
P. D. James
Quintin Jardine
Donna Leon
Jill McGown
William McIlvanney

Magdalen Nabb
Janet Neel
Iain Pears
Mike Phillips
Ian Rankin
Ruth Rendell
Mike Ripley
Minette Walters
Robert Wilson

COMIC BRITISH

Simon Brett
Ruth Dudley Edwards
Jonathan Gash
Mike Ripley
Simon Shaw

BRITISH POLICE PROCEDURALS

W. J. Burley
Colin Dexter
John Harvey
Reginald Hill
Bill James
Quintin Jardine
R. D. Wingfield

PSYCHOLOGICAL DRAMA

Jane Adams
Frances Fyfield
Patricia Highsmith
Elizabeth Ironside
P. D. James
Ingrid Noll
Ruth Rendell
Georges Simenon
Julian Symons
Andrew Taylor
Barbara Vine
Minette Walters

AMERICAN CLASSICS

W. R. Burnett
James M. Cain

Raymond Chandler
Erle Stanley Gardner
Dashiell Hammett
Chester Himes
Ross MacDonald
Margaret Millar
Rex Stout

PULP CLASSICS

David Goodis
Horace McCoy
John D. McDonald
Mickey Spillane
Jim Thompson
Charles Willeford
Cornell Woolrich

CONTEMPORARY AMERICAN NOIR

Lawrence Block
Edward Bunker
James Lee Burke
Robert Campbell
Jerome Charyn
Michael Connelly
James Crumley
Stephen Dobyns
James Ellroy
Loren Estleman
James Hall
William Hjorstberg
Craig Holden
Eugene Izzi
Joe Lansdale
Arthur Lyons
Walter Mosley
George Pelecanos
Sam Reaves
James Sallis
Richard Stark
Charles Willeford
Daniel Woodrell

MODERN AMERICAN

Paula Gosling
Lawrence Gough
Sue Grafton
Joseph Hansen
George V. Higgins
Tony Hillerman
Faye Kellerman
Jonathan Kellerman
Laurie King
Elmore Leonard
Sharyn McCrumb
Carol O'Connell
Doug J. Swanson
Andrew Vachss

NOIR GROTESQUE

Robert Ferrigno
James Hall
Carl Hiaasen
William Hjorstberg
Joe Lansdale

AMERICAN POLICE PROCEDURAL

Ed McBain
Joseph Wambaugh

AMERICAN COMIC

Lawrence Block
Janet Evanovich
Kinky Friedman
Carl Hiaasen
Elmore Leonard
Robet B. Parker
Lawrence Sanders
Lawrence Shames
Doug J. Swanson
Donald E. Westlake

EUROPEAN CRIME

Jakob Arjouni
Delacorta
Nicholas Freeling
Sebasatien Japrisot
Manuel Vazquez Montalban
Ingrid Noll
Daniel Pennac
Georges Simenon
Josef Skvorecky

FEMALE PRIVATE EYES AND HEROINES

Linda Barnes
Liza Cody
Patricia Cornwell
Amanda Cross
Stella Duffy
Sarah Dunant
Sue Grafton
Lauren Henderson
Karen Kijewski
Val McDermid
Marcia Muller
Carol O'Connell
Sara Paretsky
Sandra Scoppettone
Gillian Slovo
Joan Smith

THRILLERS

Lionel Davidson
Philip Kerr
Reggie Nadelson
James Patterson
A. J. Quinnell
Julian Rathbone
Ross Thomas
Scott Turow

BLACK CRIME WRITING

Clarence Cooper Jr
Victor Headley
Chester Himes
Iceberg Slim
Walter Mosley
Charles Perry
Mike Phillips

HISTORICAL

Michael Clynes
Lindsey Davis
P. C. Doherty
Elizabeth Eyre
Robert Van Gulik
Paul Harding
Michael Jecks
A. E. Marston
Ian Morson
Amy Myers
Michael Pearce
Anne Perry
Ellis Peters
Candace Robb
Kate Ross
Kate Sedley
Peter Tremayne

GAY CRIME WRITING

Sarah Dreher
Stella Duffy
Joseph Hansen
Val McDermid
Sandra Scoppettone
Mary Wings

RACING CRIME

Stephen Dobyns
Dick Francis
John Francome

Services *at* Waterstone's

THE PRICE PROMISE

If you find any book cheaper locally we shall happily refund the difference (ask a bookseller for details).

BOOKSEARCH

If the book you want is no longer in print, Waterstone's Booksearch Service will try to locate a second-hand copy for you. Booksearch, 32-40 Calverley Road, Tunbridge Wells, TN1 2TD (fax 01892 521 400).

MAIL ORDER

We can send any book in print to anywhere in the world. Orders over £45 within the United Kingdom are sent post-free. Waterstone's Mailing Service, 4-5 Milsom Street, Bath BA1 1DA (tel 01225 448 595; fax 01225 444 732 or 01225 420 575).

SIGNED FIRST EDITIONS

Waterstone's Signed First Editions Collection offers a choice of up to 150 of the year's finest fiction and non-fiction titles – all signed by the author and posted to you for a subscription of only £6. Waterstone's Signed First Editions Collection, 4-5 Milsom Street, Bath BA1 1DA (tel 01225 448 595; fax 01225 444 732 or 01225 420 575).

BOOK VOUCHERS

Accepted in over 500 bookshops in the United Kingdom and Ireland, including all branches of Waterstone's and WH Smith. As well as posting them anywhere in the world, we provide a card free of charge.

WRAPPING, ORDERING AND POSTING

Most branches will happily gift-wrap your book in a choice of papers. If the book you are looking for is unavailable in the branch, we can order it for you and even post it to any destination in the world.

WATERSTONE'S RECOMMENDS

All the books in a Waterstone's bookshop are bought and selected by the booksellers working in the branch. No matter the subject, please ask for their advice or look out for the Book of the Month or our monthly selection of the best new books – Waterstone's Recommends.

WATERSTONE'S BOOKSHOP ON THE INTERNET

Order any book securely by credit card to be delivered direct to your door or anywhere around the world and join our on-line club at www.waterstones.co.uk

W MAGAZINE

Waterstone's own literary quarterly, available from all branches, price £1.

Where to find your nearest Waterstone's

ABERDEEN
236 Union Street
Tel: 01224 571655

BATH
4–5 Milsom Street
Tel: 01225 448515

University of Bath
Claverton Down
Tel: 01225 465565

BELFAST
Queen's Building
8 Royal Avenue
Tel: 01232 247355

BIRMINGHAM
24–26 High St
Tel: 0121 633 4353

BOLTON *(Nov 1997)*
32-36 Deansgate

BOURNEMOUTH
14/16 The Arcade
Tel: 01202 299449

BRADFORD
University of Bradford
Great Holton Road
Tel: 01274 727885

Management Centre Bookshop,
Emm Lane
Tel: 01274 481404

The Wool Exchange
Tel: 01274 723127

BRIGHTON
55–56 North Street
Tel: 01273 327867

BRISTOL
27–29 College Green
Tel: 0117 925 0511

Computer Centre
University of Bristol
Tyndall Avenue
Tel: 0117 925 4297

The Galleries Broadmead
Tel: 0117 925 2274

BROMLEY
20-22 Market Square
Tel: 0181 464 6562

CAMBRIDGE
6 Bridge Street
Tel: 01223 300123

CANTERBURY
20 St Margaret's St
Tel: 01227 456343

CARDIFF
2a The Hayes
Tel: 01222 665606

CARMARTHEN
Trinity College
Tel: 01267 238100

CHELTENHAM
88–90 The Promenade
Tel: 01242 512722

CHESTER
43–45 Bridge
Street Row
Tel: 01244 328040

COLCHESTER
16 Culver Precinct
Tel: 01206 767623

University of Essex
Wivenhoe Park
Tel: 01206 864773

COLERAINE
Central Building
University of Ulster
Cromore Road
Tel: 01265 324 658

CORK
69 Patrick Street
Tel: 00 353 21 276522

Boole Library
University College
Tel: 00 353 21 276575

CROYDON
1063 Whitgift Centre
Tel: 0181 686 7032

DERBY
78-80 St Peter's St
Tel: 01332 296997

DORKING
54–60 South St
Tel: 01306 886884

DUBLIN
7 Dawson Street
Tel: 00 353 16 791260

The Jervis Centre
Tel: 00 353 16 8781311

DUNDEE
35 Commercial St
Tel: 01382 200322

DURHAM
69 Saddler St
Tel: 0191 383 1488

EASTBOURNE
120 Terminus Road
Tel: 01323 735676

EDINBURGH
128 Princes St
Tel: 0131 226 2666

13–14 Princes St
Tel: 0131 556 3034/5

83 George Street
Tel: 0131 225 3436

EPSOM
113 High St
Tel: 01372 741713

EXETER
48–49 High St
Tel: 01392 218392

GATESHEAD
17 The Parade
Metro Centre
Tel: 0191 493 2715

GATWICK AIRPORT
North Terminal Airside
Tel: 01293 507112

GLASGOW
45–50 Princes Square
Tel: 0141 221 9650

153–157
Sauchiehall St
Tel: 0141 332 9105

GUILDFORD
35–39 North St
Tel: 01483 302919

HANLEY
The Tontines Centre
Parliament Row
Tel: 01782 204582

HEREFORD *(Oct 1997)*
18–20 Commercial St

HULL
University of Hull
Tel: 01482 444190

The Grand Buildings,
Jameson Street
Tel: 01482 580234

INVERNESS
50–52 High St
Tel: 01463 717474

IPSWICH
15–19 Buttermarket
Tel: 01473 289044

KINGSTON-UPON-THAMES
23–25 Thames St
Tel: 0181 547 1221

LANCASTER
2–8 King St
Tel: 01524 61477

LEAMINGTON SPA
Unit 1, Priorsgate
Warwick St
Tel: 01926 883804

LEEDS
36–38 Albion St
Tel: 0113 242 0839

93–97 Albion St
Tel: 0113 244 4588

LEICESTER
21/23 High St
Tel: 0116 251 6838

LIVERPOOL
52 Bold St
Tel: 0151 709 0866

LONDON

CAMDEN, NW1
128 Camden High St
Tel: 0171 284 4948

CHARING CROSS RD, WC2
121 Charing Cross Road
Tel: 0171 434 4291

CHARING CROSS AND WESTMINSTER MEDICAL SCHOOL, W6
The Library, St Dunstans Road
Tel: 0181 748 9768

THE CITY, EC3
1 Whittington Ave
Leadenhall Market
Tel: 0171 220 7882

COVENT GARDEN, WC2
9 Garrick Street
Tel: 0171 836 6757

EARL'S COURT, SW5
266 Earl's Court Road
Tel: 0171 370 1616

GOLDSMITH'S, SE14
Goldsmith's College
New Cross
Tel: 0181 469 0262

HAMPSTEAD, NW3
68 Hampstead
High St
Tel: 0171 794 1098

HARRODS, SW1
87 Brompton Road
Tel: 0171 730 1234

IMPERIAL COLLEGE, SW7
Imperial College Road
Tel: 0171 589 3563

ISLINGTON, N1
10-12 Islington Green
Tel: 0171 704 2280

KENSINGTON, W8
193 Kensington High St
Tel: 0171 937 8432

NOTTING HILL, W11
39 Notting Hill Gate
Tel: 0171 229 9444

OLD BROMPTON RD, SW7
99 Old Brompton Road
Tel: 0171 581 8522

WIMBLEDON, SW19
12 Wimbledon Bridge
Tel: 0181 543 9899

MAIDSTONE
19 Earl Street
Tel: 01622 681112

MAILING SERVICE
Tel: 01225 448595
Fax: 01225 444732

MANCHESTER
91 Deansgate
Tel: 0161 832 1992

MIDDLESBROUGH
9 Newton Mall
Cleveland Centre
Tel: 01642 242682

University of Teeside
Middlesborough
Cleveland TS1 2NWi
Tel: 01642 242017

NEWBURY
64 Northbrook Street
Tel: 01635 569998

NEWCASTLE
104 Grey Street
Tel: 0191 261 6140

NORTHAMPTON
19 Abington Street
Tel: 01604 34854

NORWICH
21–24 Royal Arcade
Tel: 01603 632426

University of East Anglia
Tel: 01603 453625

NOTTINGHAM
1–5 Bridlesmith Gate
Tel: 0115 9484499

PERTH
St John's Centre
Tel: 01738 630013

PETERBOROUGH
6 Queensgate
Tel: 01733 313476

PLYMOUTH
65/69 New George St
Tel: 01752 256699

PRESTON
3–5 Fishergate
Tel: 01772 555766

READING
89a Broad St
Tel: 01734 581270

RICHMOND-UPON-THAMES
2–6 Hill St
Tel: 0181 332 1600

SALISBURY
7/9 High St
Tel: 01722 415596

SHEFFIELD
24 Orchard Square
Tel: 0114 272 8971

SHREWSBURY
18–19 High St
Tel: 01743 248112

SOUTHAMPTON
69 Above Bar
Tel: 01703 633130

Southampton Medical School,
Southampton General Hospital
Tel: 01703 780602

University of Southampton
Highfield
Tel: 01703 558267

SOUTHEND-ON-SEA
49–55 High St
Tel: 01702 437480

SOUTHPORT
367 Lord St
Tel: 01704 501088

STIRLING *(Oct 1997)*
Thistle Marches

STOCKPORT
103 Princes St
Tel: 0161 477 3755

STRATFORD-UPON-AVON
18 The High St
Tel: 01789 414418

SWANSEA
Oxford St
Tel: 01792 463567

SWINDON
27 Regent St
Tel: 01793 488838

TAUNTON
East St
Tel: 01823 333113

TUNBRIDGE WELLS
32/40 Calverley Road
Tel: 01892 535446

ULSTER
Central Buildings
University of Ulster
Cromoe Road
Coleraine
Tel: 01265 324 735

WATFORD
174–176 The Harlequin Centre,
High St
Tel: 01923 218197

WINCHESTER
1/2 Kings Walk
Tel: 01962 866206

WORCESTER
95 High St
Tel: 01905 723397

YORK
28–29 High Ousegate
Tel: 01904 628740